CHARLTON HESTON

CHARLTON HESTON

A Pyramid Illustrated History of the Movies

by
MICHAEL B. DRUXMAN

General Editor: TED SENNETT

PUBLICATIONS
NEW YORK

In memory of my mother

CHARLTON HESTON
A Pyramid Illustrated History of the Movies

Pyramid edition published October 1976

Library of Congress Catalog Card Number: 76-41108

Printed in the United States of America

Pyramid Books are published by Pyramid Publications (Harcourt Brace Jovanovich, Inc.). Its trademarks, consisting of the word "Pyramid" and the portrayal of a pyramid, are registered in the United States Patent Office.

PYRAMID PUBLICATIONS
(Harcourt Brace Jovanovich, Inc.)
757 Third Avenue, New York, N.Y. 10017

(graphic design by anthony basile)

ACKNOWLEDGMENTS

Grateful acknowledgment is made to the many individuals and organizations who gave of their time, their knowledge, and/or loaned films for viewing purposes:

Academy of Motion Picture Arts and Sciences, Michael Ansara, Audio Brandon Films, The British Film Institute, Budget Films, Films, Inc., Tom Gries, KHJ-TV, KTTV, Henry Levin, Christopher Mitchum, George Thomas, Twentieth Century-Fox, United Artists Corporation, Universal Pictures, King Vidor, Jessica Walter, and Albert Zugsmith.

Photographs: Jerry Vermilye, The Memory Shop, Gene Andrewski, Cinemabilia, Movie Star News, P.B.S. Archives, and the companies that produced and distributed the films of Charlton Heston.

CONTENTS

Introduction 11

The Pre-Hollywood Years 15

Paramount and DeMille 28

The Two Big Ones 57

A Heap of Epics 81

It's Nice to Work Regular 102

The Upward Swing 127

Bibliography 143

The Films of Charleton Heston 145

Index 153

As Moses in THE TEN COMMANDMENTS (1956)

INTRODUCTION

Charlton Heston is a dedicated actor who enjoys discussing his craft and, as such, has often been invited to address student groups of aspiring performers. To illustrate a point to these audiences, he will often recall a minor incident that occurred while he was on location in the Black Hills of South Dakota for *The Savage* (1952), his third Hollywood production and first Western.

One scene in the film called for Heston to race his horse down a slope—past Indian extras and buffalo—and stop in front of the camera to deliver a single line. It was a simple piece of dialogue, but the serious young actor insisted on proposing a rather intricate reading to the director, George Marshall. This show business veteran listened patiently to his star's dissertation, then replied, "Look, kid, in this business, the most important thing is not whether you act, but can you ride a horse to your mark."

It was a good piece of advice—one that Charlton Heston has followed in the broadest sense during his more than 2½ decades on the Hollywood scene. Respected and well liked by his peers, he has garnered an international reputation as a capable leading man who not only approaches his job in a thoroughly professional manner, but is also deeply interested in improving the movie industry as a whole, through his work with the Screen Actors' Guild, the American Film Institute, and the Academy of Motion Picture Arts and Sciences.

Albert Zugsmith, producer of the revered, Orson Welles-directed *Touch of Evil* (1958), describes Heston as "a thinking actor . . . a nice man, but of greater importance, a 'team player' who makes no waves during production."

Amid today's ever-increasing movie-making costs, an actor with a cooperative spirit is much more appealing to a producer than one with a more temperamental nature—a basic reason why Heston, despite his questionable *personal* following at the box office, finds himself regularly employed.

He has starred in some of the most successful pictures to ever adorn theater screens; in fact, three of them—*The Ten Commandments* (1956), *Ben-Hur* (1959), and *Earthquake* (1974)—according to *Variety*'s 1976 listing, are among the twenty all-time top grossing pictures, ranking fourteenth, eighteenth, and twentieth respectively. Indeed, the trade paper reports that, thus far, sixteen of Heston's movies have made its definitive list of box-office champions which have grossed $4 million or more in domestic rentals.

His impressive list of credits notwithstanding, Heston has never been considered by his industry to be truly viable when it comes to attracting patrons to the box office. One only need scan the list of his most successful films—*The Greatest Show on Earth* (1952), *El Cid* (1961), *Planet of the Apes* (1968), *The Three Musketeers* (1974), and *Airport 1975* (1974), as well as the three aforementioned hits—to see that these productions, because of their spectacle, special effects, all-star casts, or other unique qualities, were already endowed with a high audience appeal and did not really depend on *his* presence for their ultimate prosperity. Conversely, many of his other films, including the movie containing his best performance to date—*Will Penny* (1968)—died in the theaters, despite, in several instances, above average and even superior critical reviews. Lacking extraordinary elements with which to lure the public, these films depended too much on Heston's name for their financial rewards and, unfortunately, that proved not enough.

Perhaps his inability to attract a large personal cortege stems from the fact that, on the screen—with a few notable exceptions—Heston appears stiff and projects little warmth or vulnerability. An actress

he's worked with refers to him as "the world's highest paid nonactor," and another critic tags him "the grimacer." His stiffness works well when he is playing a hardnosed military man, a stoic historical figure, or a bigger-than-life fictional hero; however, in a love scene, he usually appears as wooden as a cigar-store Indian.

Within a more than adequate range, he is, most certainly, a good, effective actor who has provided audiences with many telling dramatic moments. Who better than Heston—with his 6'2" Adonis-like frame—could have landed that crippled plane in *Airport 1975*; held off the Boxers in *55 Days at Peking* (1963); or destroyed the army of marauding ants in *The Naked Jungle* (1954). In the role of the cool, determined, "invincible" super-hero, he has few equals.

In the twenties and thirties, George Arliss and then Paul Muni were given the bulk of the movies' biographical assignments, yet the number of contributions Heston has made to this genre dwarfs the combined real-life portrayals of both these fine actors. Over the years, Heston has essayed—with varying degrees of success—such pontifical characters as Andrew Jackson (twice), Moses, John the Baptist, Michelangelo, General Charles "Chinese" Gordon, and Cardinal Richelieu, among others.

As Taylor in PLANET OF THE APES (1968)

("I seem to have a face that belongs earlier than the 20th century," he explains. "Perhaps the further back the better.")

He will go to great lengths to research each of his roles and, as a result of this extensive preparation, has seldom delivered a performance that was less than equal to the particular screenplay he was enacting. Missing, perhaps, was that extra spark of charisma . . . an undefinable charm which is present in only the most popular of screen personalities. With even some of his better portrayals, one can't help wondering if another actor, endowed with a more flexible on-camera technique, might not have played the part more interestingly.

In his defense, director William Wyler has said: "The most extraordinary quality that Chuck Heston brings to his performance is his devotion to the job of being an actor, coupled with keeping that devotion from being dull. Unlike certain other actors, who shall remain nameless, he knows that a handsome face is not enough to win and hold a star's reputation."

Although he is still far from the ideal, Heston has, in all fairness, improved as an actor during the last few years, underplaying his more recent roles in a refreshingly relaxed manner. His association with a lengthy list of screen successes has, undeniably, made him a "prestige" star in both Hollywood and the world, and if his name cannot "make" a marquee, it can certainly enhance it. This, coupled with his keen ability to recognize a good screen property when he sees it and his not being afraid to take chances on a more thoughtful piece of literary material, such as *The War Lord* (1965) or *Soylent Green* (1973), should insure his prominent participation in important motion pictures for many years to come.

He was born Charlton Carter on October 4, 1924, in Evanston, Illinois, a town of about 80,000 people, located on the shores of Lake Michigan. His father, Russell Carter, came from a logging family that owned and worked a large mass of timberland in Roscommon County in Michigan; his mother was the former Lilla Charlton of Chicago. Both parents were of English-Scottish descent.

When "Chuck" was quite young, the Carter clan, which was later to include a brother, Alan, and sister, Lilla, moved to the tiny northwoods hamlet of St. Helen, Michigan. There, in this isolated community, the boy learned to hunt and fish and, because there were no children his own age in the area, spent much of his time acting out stories his father would read to him. ("I cannot remember a time when I didn't want to be an actor," he recalls.)

Of course, with a name like Charlton, getting along with other children was not an easy task, especially after his first day of school when the unknowing teacher requested, "Would our new little girl, Charlotte, please stand up?"

His dramatic career began at the age of five in St. Helen's one-room schoolhouse. It was the annual Christmas pageant and he had the starring role—Santa Claus. "Another actor in the family," was the

THE PRE-HOLLYWOOD YEARS

prediction of great-uncle Percy Charlton, himself a thespian.

Charlton was nine when his parents divorced. ("It was an extremely traumatic experience and it colored my whole adolescence. . . . For years it seemed an awful thing to me. I felt a deep sense of personal guilt.") Lilla soon remarried—a mill operator named Chester Heston—and, shortly thereafter, with the three Carter children assuming their goodhearted stepfather's name, the newly formed family moved back to Evanston. Later, Chuck would be enrolled in New Trier High School in nearby Winnetka—an institution at which he was very unhappy. As he told the *Saturday Evening Post* in 1965: "It was so remote up in Michigan that, when I first returned, I remember being actually scared to death of the automobile traffic and the noise and everything else that goes with a big city. It was a social kind of school, and I had never even learned to dance. And kids are the most conventional people in the world. It is more important than anything else for them to conform, and I was a kind of oddball. I was driven into being independent. The fact that,

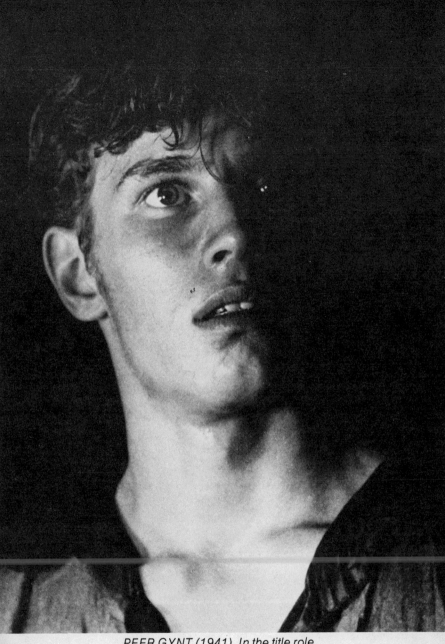

PEER GYNT (1941). In the title role

until sixteen, I was small for my age, made it worse because I was the most awkward guy in school."

New Trier did have an excellent drama training program and the shy Charlton took full advantage of its facilities to develop the strong interest he'd always had in the field. He took various classes, played leads in many productions, and, as a result, won an acting scholarship to Northwestern University.

To support himself at college, the now-lanky Heston did a variety of odd jobs, including operating an apartment-house elevator on the night shift. Eventually, he would earn extra dollars as an actor on Chicago radio, his rich voice being heard on many soap operas, as well as on the adventure serial, "Terry and the Pirates."

Heston's classmates in Northwestern's School of Speech included such future luminaries as Patricia Neal, Ralph Meeker, and a talented young man named David Bradley, who had previously attended the Todd School at Woodstock, Illinois—the same private institution where Orson Welles had studied.

Bradley loved filmmaking and, after leaving Todd, where he made a movie called *The Three Friends*, produced, photographed and acted in a number of self-financed 16mm productions, such as *Treasure Island, Oliver Twist*, and *A Christmas Carol*—all made in and around Chicago. At Northwestern in 1941, he enlisted the aid of fellow students in mounting his ambitious ninety-minute version of Ibsen's *Peer Gynt*, casting seventeen-year-old Charlton Heston in the title role of the irresponsible, superficial youth of Norse folklore who travels the globe to seek his fortune.

Cleverly mixing stock footage of scenic Norway, Arabs racing across the desert, and a miniature sailing ship caught in a Hollywood-manufactured storm, with scenes shot in the woods of Wisconsin and on the shores of Lake Michigan, Bradley, with a minimum of money, was able to create a reasonably believable picture of Norway and Morocco in the nineteenth century. The technical aspects of this black-and-white,* largely silent production were often primitive, but the director did exhibit a flair for creative lighting and photography, reminiscent of Orson Welles' early picture work. Indeed, there were instances where Bradley's style was almost too clever, in that he would employ a shot that was unique for its own sake, yet a distraction from the film as a whole.

The movie contained only one short section of dialogue, supplemented by far too many title cards

---

* A short fantasy sequence was, at various times, tinted either green, blue, or red.

17

PEER GYNT (1941). With Kathryne Elfstrom

than necessary to tell the story. A poorly recorded, loosely synchronized rendition of Edvard Grieg's *Peer Gynt* score served as the production's principal soundtrack. Acting, in general, did not rise above a college level, and the scenario, for one not familiar with the classical tale, was sometimes unclear.

Considering the paltry circumstances under which *Peer Gynt* was made, Heston did rather well in his part, aging from a boyish, conceited young man to the frightened, defeated adult who, near the film's conclusion, begs the ominous Button Molder to spare his life. There's some exaggerated teeth-gritting in the performance and, at times, he appears to be playing a scene without really understanding its motivation, but, generally his portrayal, like Bradley's direction, gives promise of better things to come.

Heston had gone out for freshman football at Northwestern ("I was not a distinguished player even in high school, but I was either cocky enough or stupid enough to try the game at this University, which plays in a fairly rough league."); however after he'd broken his nose in a scrimmage, he decided to forsake the sport and concentrate more fully on his dramatic studies. What he didn't realize at the time was that that

smashed piece of cartilage would, years later, prove to be a vital factor in his garnering one of the most important roles of his motion-picture career.

Another aspiring dramatic student at the University was an attractive, dark-haired girl named Lydia Clarke—the daughter of a high-school principal—who hailed from Two Rivers, Wisconsin. As did many of the young people on campus, she had a job when she wasn't attending classes—working in the college cafeteria.

Sitting behind her during their class in "Fundamental Theatre," Charlton was quite taken with Miss Clarke, yet his shyness prevented him from asking her out—until, one day, she asked his advice on how she should read a particular line of dialogue in a scene she was rehearsing. Seizing this opportunity to get better acquainted with the lovely nineteen-year-old, Chuck invited her to the malt shop for a cup of coffee.

Heston: "At seven I'd read Ernest Thompson Seton's *Lives of the Hunted* about animals, and acted out all the parts myself. I developed a very effective wolf howl, which stood me in good stead the first time I saw Lydia."

The couple began seeing each other frequently—both in and out of the classroom. As Lydia recalled to columnist Sidney Skolsky

With wife Lydia

in 1952: "We were insufferably rude to each other during play rehearsals and argued constantly. We decided it must be love, so we got married."

Actually, it wasn't all that simple. Heston reports that he proposed regularly to his future wife on a weekly basis for a long time, but, since she was interested in a career as an actress, all he got were rejections.

She finally relented in 1944. With the war in progress, Heston had joined the Air Corps, receiving his basic training in Greensboro, North Carolina. After completing this course, he wired Lydia still another proposal and, just when he had about given up all hope, she sent her reply: "Have decided to accept your proposal."

They were married on March 17, 1944—St. Patrick's Day—in a Greensboro chapel. After the wedding, Chuck was transferred to Selfridge Field near Detroit for instruction as a radio operator. Ultimately, he was sent overseas to serve with the 11th Air Force in the Aleutians, mostly working the radio on B-25s. Lydia, in the meantime, continued her studies at Northwestern.

JULIUS CAESAR (1949). As Marc Antony

JULIUS CAESAR (1949). With unidentified actor

Following the war, Heston returned briefly to school and, while there, designed the costumes for David Bradley's most expensive film to date—a $5 thousand sound production of *Macbeth*. The 73-minute "epic," shot on weekends during 1946 in Winnetka and Racine, starred Bradley in the title role.

Heston was restless after his discharge—anxious to get to New York and try his luck at the theatrical career he'd always dreamed of. Despite entreaties from friends that he wait and finish his education, so that he could fall back on teaching if he were unsuccessful, the determined young man departed for the big city, arriving with his wife in the midst of a housing shortage.

He was a veteran, however, and because of that status, the couple was able to secure a thirty-dollar-a-month cold water flat in the heart of "Hell's Kitchen."

Heston began making the rounds of theatrical casting offices. He was twenty-two and eager to work, but, unfortunately, there was no interest in hiring this strapping youth. To pay the bills, Lydia did some modeling. "We never starved," reflects Heston, "but we weren't far from it occasionally."

When he did find a job, it was for both Hestons—as co-directors and performers at the Thomas Wolfe Memorial Theatre in Asheville, North Carolina, later renamed the Asheville Community Theatre. Heston remembers: "We went there to do one play, earn a little money and then return to New York. It was a pleasant thing, after having been thrown out of countless offices and having doors slammed in my face, to go somewhere an opinion was respected and you could *work*." Rather than the one play they'd been contracted for, the couple did a total of six productions in Asheville, including *The Glass Menagerie, Kiss and Tell*, and *State of the Union*.

Two days after his return to New York in 1947, Heston obtained the role of "Proculeius," Caesar's lieutenant, in Katharine Cornell's production of Shakespeare's *Antony and Cleopatra*, which opened at the Martin Beck Theatre on November 26th. The star's husband, Guthrie McClintic, directed the play, which featured Eli Wallach, Maureen Stapleton, and Bruce Gordon in secondary roles. Heston later remarked: "I'm sure I got the job because I'm over six feet. Miss Cornell is a tall woman and likes tall actors around."

The summer of 1948 found Charlton and Lydia working in a Mt. Gretna, Pennsylvania, stock company, playing leads in shows like *You Can't Take It With You, Angel Street*, and *John Loves Mary*.

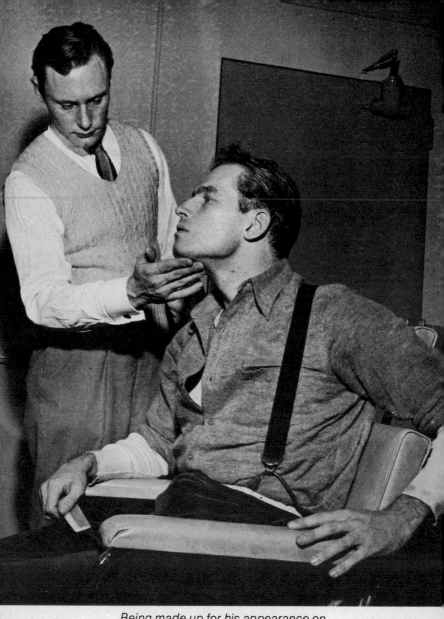

Being made up for his appearance on television in A DAY IN TOWN (1953)

There were two more Broadway plays for Heston in 1949. Both were failures. *Leaf and Bough*, written by Joseph Hayes, and staged by Rouben Mamoulian, opened on January 21st at the Cort, with a cast that included Richard Hart, Coleen Gray, and David White. John Chapman of the *Daily News* tagged it "the best-acted, best-lighted, best-set radio serial I ever saw, with never a trick missed in script or production." Heston had the role of Glenn Campbell, and of his contribution, *The New York Sun* said: "Charlton Heston holds your interest as the repulsive and despicable brother."

On February 27th, he opened at the Lenox Hill Playhouse in *Cock-a-Doodle-Doo*, a new play by Iris Tree. Dismissed as "gibberish" by *The New York Times*, the show also featured Darren McGavin, Katherine Squire, and John Fiedler. Heston's role was that of "Az."

That same year, Heston traveled back to Northwestern to star in another David Bradley production. The ninety-minute sound movie was Shakespeare's *Julius Caesar*, and it starred Heston as Marc Antony and director Bradley as Brutus. The budget on the black-and-white picture was a "staggering" $11 thousand.

Remaining fairly faithful to Shakespeare's text, *Julius Caesar* was a fascinating little film—not so much for its technical aspects or its performances, both of which were sorely deficient, but because of Bradley's imaginative use of existing buildings in the Chicago area in presenting an acceptable re-creation of early Rome. Filming against the Rosenwald Museum, Soldiers Field, and other landmarks in that vast Midwestern city, Bradley, in his Wellesian style, seldom utilized a long shot, thereby camouflaging his meagre production values by symbolizing his action in small parts—a section of a crowd, a section of a battle, and so forth. A few individual sequences in the generally slow-moving film —such as the murder of Caesar—were played very effectively.

Costumes were homemade and the actors, for the most part, came from the Northwestern Speech Department. One of the leaders in the crowd scenes would later have a moderately successful Hollywood career under the name of Jeffrey Hunter.

Heston's performance, though slightly wooden, was, nevertheless, a competent reading of Antony, lacking nuances, but clearly the most professional rendition in the picture. Bradley, on the other hand, gave audiences a rather stoic Brutus, paying scant attention to the noble conspirator's inner turmoil.

Nationally released by Brandon Films in 1952, Bradley's production won the award for best film at the Locarno Film Festival in 1953. Heston gave an interview to the *Los Angeles Times* about that time, in which he discussed his feelings about the Bard: "Shakespearean roles supply a routine not unlike the 'Seven Ages of Man' soliloquy from *As You Like It*. You have to grow into them at certain well-defined intervals. You can play Marc Antony at an earlier age than Brutus, for example, and then Macbeth at a still later age, while naturally King Lear can come as the culmination of your maturity.

"Shakespeare spells completeness to me in the opportunities that he affords an actor through his lifetime, and I will never be happy, I am sure, without essaying one play or another from time to time. What is more, I like to work on the stage."

Heston went back to the stage shortly after he completed his scenes in *Julius Caesar*, appearing on Broadway in another flop —*Design for a Stained Glass Window*, by William Berney and Howard Richardson. Directed by Ella Gerber, the play opened at the Mansfield Theatre on January 23, 1950 and starred Martha Scott. Though critics considered the production plodding and pretentious, Heston, as John Clitherow, received good notices, as evidenced by Robert Garland in the *Journal-American*: "Charlton Heston . . . is an assured and personable young actor . . ."

Like so many New York actors, Heston had benefited greatly by the advent of television in the late forties and was, indeed, one of the first freelance performers to achieve success in that new medium, playing leads in live dramatic shows like "Studio One": "When I started to do television, theatrical actors of any reputation wouldn't do it because it didn't pay anything, and film actors were contractually prohibited from doing TV. So I was competing with actors in my own category—out of work!"

On television, he played in such productions as *Wuthering Heights* (as Heathcliff), *Of Human Bondage*, and *Jane Eyre* (as Rochester). This latter adaptation, which featured Mary Sinclair in the title role, was seen by movie producer Hal Wallis who was so impressed with Heston's portrayal that he signed the twenty-five-year-old actor—without a screen test—to a nonexclusive personal contract.

Heston headed for Hollywood to make his first film, but Lydia wasn't with him. She'd also gotten a major career break and was appearing in the Chicago company of *Detective Story*.

Arriving on the West Coast, Heston signed in at Paramount—the studio Wallis had been aligned with since 1945—to star in *Dark City* (1950), a low-budget melodrama based on a story by Larry Marcus and adapted for the screen by Ketti Frings. Marcus, along with John Meredyth Lucas, had written the final screenplay. The veteran William Dieterle directed it.

The rather intriguing story dealt with three professional gamblers (Heston, Jack Webb, and Ed Begley), who cheat an out-of-town sucker (Don DeFore) out of money entrusted to him for another purpose. When the victim commits suicide, his maniacal brother (Mike Mazurki with a dubbed voice) stalks the trio of shady characters, murdering two of them before he is apprehended as he tries to strangle Heston in a Las Vegas motel.

Endowed with some effective performances and truly chilling moments (such as the scene in which Heston—gun in hand—waits for Mazurki in his motel room, not knowing the madman is already hiding in the closet), *Dark City* was nevertheless, flawed by indifferent direction and a screenplay that diluted the plot's suspense by including too many superfluous scenes in which the star is romancing one of his two leading ladies—Lizabeth Scott (a night-

PARAMOUNT AND DEMILLE

club singer) and Viveca Lindfors (DeFore's widow). These episodes may have told audiences a bit more about what made Heston's moody character "tick," but they also gave a relaxed quality to what should have been a tightly paced production.

Heston, though a bit formal in many of his scenes, did deliver an adequate reading of what was a rather bland character in the first place. As might be expected, the critics' reaction to his *professional* film debut in this disappointing "B" movie was on the neutral side. *Variety* commented: "Heston is capable in the lead, but the spot, as developed, is not quite socko enough to back up the enthusiasm of producer Hal Wallis. The jury will be out on Heston until his next film is released." *The New York Times* called his performance "perfectly acceptable" but was unimpressed with the role and the film. Bosley Crowther called him "a tall, tweedy, roughhewn sort of chap who looks like a triple-threat halfback on a midwestern college football team."

Heston's reflections on the project: "It burned down no cities. I played a role Bill Holden really should have had. If he'd played that

28

DARK CITY (1950). With Lizabeth Scott

part, it would have been a great picture."

After this ineffective debut, the actor was anything but "in demand" with Hollywood producers. Certainly he was a virile, handsome leading man with a fair amount of talent, but in the tenuous fifties, when filmmakers were fighting to stay alive at the box office, nobody was about to entrust even a medium-budget picture to a performer who had not shown that he had some sort of following.

Thus, Heston returned to New York to work for "tinsel-town's" prime opposition—television. During the next few months, he did a number of top live dramatic shows, including "Philco Playhouse,"

"Suspense," and "Studio One." On this latter program, he played Petruchio to Lisa Kirk's Katherine in *The Taming of the Shrew* (June 5, 1950) and co-starred with Judith Evelyn in Joseph Liss' production of *Macbeth* (October 20, 1951). An exacting man—especially when it comes to analyzing his own performances—Heston told interviewer Pete Martin in 1960: "When I did the TV version of *Macbeth*, I was told, 'Do you realize that more people saw you play Macbeth than all the actors who ever played Macbeth put together?' My answer was, 'Yes, but how good did I play it?' Quantity is not the best yardstick."

He still had his obligations to

DARK CITY (1950). With Viveca Lindfors

Wallis, who would ultimately sell the actor's contract to Paramount. Unfortunately, neither the producer nor the studio really knew what to do with their new property.

Heston was back in Los Angeles for awhile, tending to some publicity matters on the Paramount lot, when he was introduced to Cecil B. DeMille. "When he met small fry like myself," the performer recalls, "he was gracious, but seldom remembered you. One day I was driving past the gate where his bungalow was, and he was standing on the steps talking to a group of his people. I smiled at him and waved, and he waved back, not having the foggiest notion who I was. He turned to his secretary and asked who I was, and she replied, 'Charlton Heston. You saw his picture, *Dark City*, in the screening room last week and didn't like it.'

"DeMille thought for a moment and said, 'Somehow he looks different today. He looks cheerful . . . a sort of friendly look to him.

In the early fifties

On the set of THE GREATEST SHOW ON EARTH (1952). With Betty Hutton, Cornel Wilde, and Cecil B. DeMille

He might be good as the circus manager in *The Greatest Show on Earth*."

The producer/director summoned Heston to his office for a series of long conferences . . . each one consisting of his telling the actor the entire story of his upcoming circus epic from the viewpoint of the character for which Heston was being considered: "He took an hour to tell me about my part. It was as if I were an interviewer who had asked him, 'Tell me what your next picture is all about, Mr. DeMille.'

"I went to see him a half dozen times and at the end of each conference I'd say, 'That's a marvelous role, Mr. DeMille.' And, he would say, 'It was nice of you to come in.' "

Having by now, rented an inexpensive Los Angeles apartment (while maintaining his thirty-dollar-a-month flat in New York), Heston was kept in suspense by the prestigious filmmaker for several weeks. Though DeMille never asked him to read or test, he wanted to confer with Heston on a number of occasions so he could be sure in his own mind that this was the right actor for the all-important assignment.

About two weeks after the last meeting, Heston received word through his agents that DeMille had made up his mind and chosen him. This was the break every actor longs for—an *important* role in an *important* picture.

The Greatest Show on Earth

THE GREATEST SHOW ON EARTH (1952). As Brad

THE GREATEST SHOW ON EARTH (1952).
With James Stewart and Cornel Wilde

(1952) was a mammoth production in the DeMille manner, crammed with real-life acts from the Ringling Brothers, Barnum & Bailey circus, as well as enough glamour and thrills to satisfy any family audience. Surely no motion picture dealing with circus life has ever matched this magnificent Technicolor tribute.

Filmed over a six-month period on the Paramount lot and in Florida at Ringling Brothers' winter quarters, the production was, as were most DeMille epics, flawed with an often juvenile script by Fredric M. Frank, Barre Lyndon, and Theodore St. John, containing trite dialogue ("You have nothing but sawdust in your veins") and two-dimensional characters.

The action moved slowly at times, due to some stagnant "dramatic" sequences, but when DeMille switched his story back to the glitter and tension of the center ring, the public was more than satisfied. The climax of the picture was a gigantic train wreck—one of the most exciting action sequences ever recorded on celluloid.

Heston received third billing in the all-star cast (after Betty Hutton and Cornel Wilde), although his role of the tough circus manager, who was principally concerned with making sure the show opened in the next town, was actually the story's pivotal character. This was one time when the often starched quality of Heston's acting technique worked well for him, making his

THE SAVAGE (1952). With Joan Taylor

portrayal one of the most convincing in the movie. Also contributing fine performances were James Stewart as a clown who is wanted for murder, and Gloria Grahame as the heartless assistant to a jealous elephant trainer (played with a phony accent by Lyle Bettger).

The Academy Award for Best Picture of the Year was presented to *The Greatest Show on Earth*, and it eventually achieved a domestic gross of $14 million. More important for Heston, it made the powers at Paramount realize that they had a viable new star under contract, and various producers began developing projects especially for him.

Heston's favorite compliment on the DeMille film came from a woman whose letter praised the performances of the rest of the cast, then added: "I think it's amazing the way the circus manager fitted in with the professional actors."

His first post-DeMille assignment was in an entertaining, if forgettable, Indians-versus-Cavalry outdoor action film from Paramount, entitled *The Savage* (original title: *Warbonnet*). Released in September of 1952, the Technicolor production, directed by George Marshall, was filmed amid the scenic Black Hills of South Dakota. The screenplay was by Sydney Boehm, based on a novel by L. L. Foreman.

Heston played a white man who, as a small boy, had been rescued by the Sioux after a Crow war party had wiped out the wagon train in which he had been traveling west with his father. Raised by the Indians, he is forced to take a stand as either redskin or white when soldiers are ordered to move the Sioux to reservations.

Though the film had a well-woven plot, sections of the Indian dialogue were childish—a throwback to the "White man speak with forked tongue" school of drama. In spite of this, however, the Indians were presented with considerable dignity as intelligent, sensitive members of a proud race, who were fighting for survival.

Again, Heston's staid screen personality—complete with occasional grimaces—was exactly what the character of Warbonnet needed for believability. It was an effective portrayal, particularly in a scene where he wrestles with his conscience in deciding whether he should lead a wagon train full of women and children into a Sioux ambush. The actor also had an interesting piece of business earlier in the film when, visiting the army fort, he views through the window couples dancing at a Saturday night social. Unaccustomed to the ways of civilization, he makes a feeble attempt to copy the dance steps, until he is joined on the porch by heroine

RUBY GENTRY (1952). With Jennifer Jones

RUBY GENTRY (1952). With Jennifer Jones

Susan Morrow, who tutors him to the point where he can join in the recreation.

At another spot in the action, Milburn Stone, who was effective as a crusty old cavalry sergeant, asked Heston: "Don't you ever smile?" Unfortunately, if one stretches the point a bit, this line would be appropriate for most of Heston's early pictures.

Following *The Savage*, he moved over to Twentieth Century-Fox to co-star with Jennifer Jones and Karl Malden in *Ruby Gentry* (1952), a film directed by King Vidor from a screenplay by Sylvia Richards. (The story credit went to Arthur Fitz-Richard.) In the title role, Miss Jones played a girl of questionable reputation who marries the richest man in town (Malden), then, after his accidental death, uses his wealth to destroy the people who snubbed her and accused her of murdering her husband. At the head of her list of victims is Boake Tackman (Heston), the man she truly loves, but who had thrown her over for a girl on the "right side of the tracks."

Director Vidor recalls that, in order to get Jennifer Jones for the lead, the producers agreed to give her husband—mogol David Selznick—cast approval. All through production, in fact, the producer of *Gone With the Wind*, who had been banished from the set, sent Vidor a steady stream of his famous memos—most of which had to do with his wife's costumes.

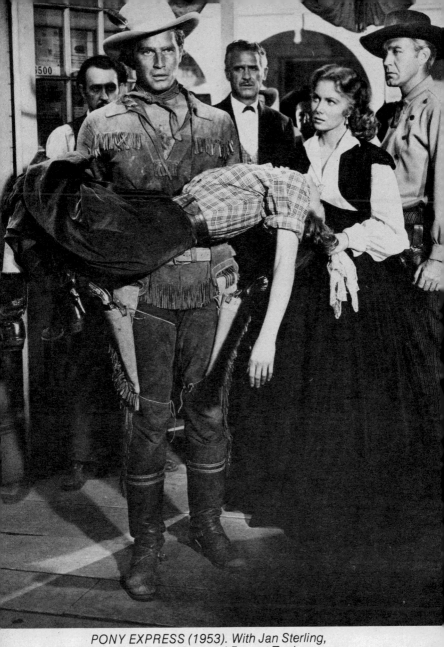

PONY EXPRESS (1953). With Jan Sterling, Rhonda Fleming, and Forrest Tucker

THE PRESIDENT'S LADY (1953). As Andrew Jackson

"What he accomplished," says the director, "was to keep Jennifer in a constant state of uncertainty."

Shot, for the most part, in California's Moro Bay area, *Ruby Gentry* proceeded without incident until, one day, the star broke her hand when she slapped Heston's face in a dramatic scene. A few minor adjustments in scheduling allowed the production to be completed without further problems.

"Heston was our first choice for the male lead," reports Vidor. "I found him to be an intelligent, capable actor who listened to direction."

The completed picture was a turgid, slow-moving melodrama, which, except for a fine, low-keyed portrayal by Malden, contained a host of overplayed performances. The sultry Miss Jones and James Anderson as her religious fanatic brother stretched their roles almost to the point of parody, and Heston, obviously uncomfortable during the love scenes, seemed even more stoic than usual. In truth, though, his written character was a mass of contradictions—a heel through most of the movie, who suddenly turns noble during the final two reels.

As with *The Savage*, there was a line of dialogue in this production which also might have fit into many of Heston's early efforts. Angered by his lack of warmth during one of their romantic interludes, Miss Jones looks at him and says: "You're always holding back!" Regrettably, that was the impression moviegoers were getting about him as well, since he was not really generating an onscreen charisma to bring life to his colorless roles.

His star definitely on the rise, however, Heston began giving interviews to fan magazines and syndicated Hollywood columnists—answering all the obligatory questions the public usually enjoys asking about the actors they are paying to see. His hobbies, for example, were listed as cartooning and painting. He would read two or three books a week when not working on a film and, of a more titillating nature, he slept in an extra-large double bed with Lydia—*without* pajamas. Instead, he wore specially-made shorts.

He owned a lodge on 172 acres in Northern Michigan, which he hoped to utilize in the future for vacations.

He approved of career wives and believed that two people could live and work together, provided both parties were interested in the other's activities. Lydia, incidentally, was continuing to accept stage assignments whenever the opportunity arose.

His favorite actor was Laurence Olivier, and he would see each of the Englishman's movies four or

THE PRESIDENT'S LADY (1953). With Susan Hayward

five times: "The guy is so good that whenever I see him on the screen, I feel like turning in my Equity card."

In 1953, audiences had the opportunity to view Heston in no less than four motion pictures, all but one of which failed to rise above programmer quality, or required him to tax his acting ability.

The first, released in March, was *Pony Express*—a Technicolor Western from Paramount. Jerry Hopper directed Charles Marquis Warren's sometimes confusing screenplay, which had been developed from a story by Frank Gruber. The main thrust of this 101-minute production was action, with little time devoted to character development. The meandering plot had Heston, as Buffalo Bill, and Forrest Tucker, as Wild Bill Hickok, acting properly heroic in their efforts to get the Pony Express through to the West Coast, despite the skulduggery of a stage-line operator and a foreign agent trying to split California from the Union. Rhonda Fleming and Jan Sterling supplied the romance, while Henry Brandon and Stuart Randall played the dastardly villains.

The President's Lady, from Twentieth Century-Fox, appeared on theater screens in May. In this film, Heston delivered one of his most relaxed performances. He was Andrew Jackson (1767-1845), and

ARROWHEAD (1953). With Jack Palance

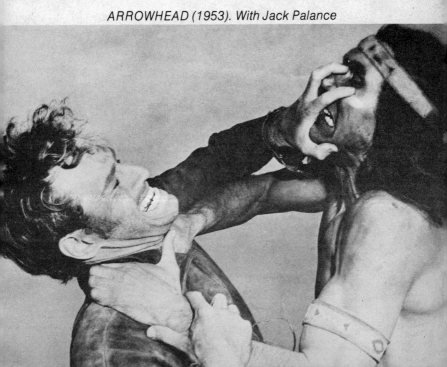

the occasionally static screenplay by John Patrick (from Irving Stone's best-selling novel) told of the President's romance with Rachel Donelson Robards, well played by Susan Hayward.

Theirs was a poignant story: When the couple was married, there was a legal error about her divorce from her first husband. Two years later, when the error was discovered, the Tennessee backwoodsman and lawyer remarried Rachel, but she was often the object of slanderous gossip (Jackson fought duels to defend her honor), and during his campaign for the presidency, his political enemies called her an adulteress. Although she died before her husband moved into the White House, she did live to hear the news of his election.

To prepare for his first film role as a historical character (Buffalo Bill in *Pony Express* was primarily a fictionalization), the actor read everything he could find on the seventh president and also asked mentor Cecil B. DeMille to screen his 1938 version of *The Buccaneer* for him, so that he could view actor Hugh Sothern's interpretation of Jackson.

The homework paid off. Heston exhibited the necessary dash for Jackson's early, more adventurous years, then aged believably to acquire the familiar roughhewn look of Old Hickory. Even more remarkable was the fact that, in his

BAD FOR EACH OTHER (1953). With Dianne Foster

intimate scenes with Miss Hayward, he displayed more sensitivity on the screen than he would again for many years. Perhaps it was the chemistry between the two performers that was responsible, or that his character was better defined than any other he had played previously, but, in any event, *The President's Lady* ranks as one of Heston's most satisfying achievements.

The film itself, though it received generally good reviews, was not without problems—the most obvious being an absence of color which would have greatly enhanced this sentimental piece of Americana.

Henry Levin, who directed the movie, recalls that it was "the last postage-stamp, black-and-white movie Fox made. While we were filming, *The Robe*—the first CinemaScope film—was in production. Darryl Zanuck saw our completed film and said: 'It's a damn good movie. Too bad it won't make a nickel. Pictures about American history never do.'"

If one had to pick the worst picture in Charlton Heston's list of credits, *Arrowhead* (1953) might not get the nod, but it would be a strong contender. The story, originally titled *Adobe Walls*, was based on an incident in the life of Al Sieber, who was the chief of Army Scouts in the Southwest United States during the Apache wars. Essentially, it told of how the experienced scout (Heston) convinces his naive superiors that a fanatical Indian warrior (Jack Palance) is planning an uprising, then leads the cavalry unit in a campaign against the marauding braves. The film ends with the two antagonists locked in hand-to-hand combat.

Not only did Charles Marquis Warren write the script for this Technicolor action movie from Paramount, but he also directed. His efforts in both areas were totally uninspired, since the film was filled with hackneyed situations, foolish dialogue, and static action sequences. It evoked no suspense whatsoever. Warren even seemed unfamiliar with basic camera and editing techniques. He played many scenes in a single master shot, thereby eliminating the reactions of characters, which may have been necessary for dramatic impact. As far as Heston and Palance were concerned, both vested their parts with such unrelenting tension that their characters became rather dull and uninteresting.

In 1950 Hal Wallis had purchased *Scalpel*, a novel by Horace McCoy, and planned to film it at Paramount with Burt Lancaster. The picture was never made, so, in 1953, Wallis assigned his rights in the property to Columbia as part of a deal by which that studio ob-

THE NAKED JUNGLE (1954). As Christopher Leiningen

tained the services of Lancaster to star in their film version of *From Here to Eternity*.

The McCoy project was retitled *Bad For Each Other* and set to appear in this programmer were Heston, Lizabeth Scott, Dianne Foster, and Lydia Clarke, playing a bit role. McCoy and Irving Wallace did the screenplay, and Irving Rapper directed.

The cliché-ridden story told of Tom Owen (Heston), a doctor from a poor coal town, who forsakes his origins in favor of a lucrative society practice which allows him little opportunity to make good use of his medical training. Following a mine cave-in, he throws over the rich girl (Scott) he had fallen for, and returns to help the people who really need him.

Heston and the other players tried valiantly to inject some life into their roles, but hampered by a script full of contradictory characters and poorly constructed scenes, not to mention the cursory direction of Mr. Rapper, they were defeated long before they even reported to the set for the first day's filming.

Aside from the work he did for DeMille, Heston's most fulfilling movie for Paramount during these early years in Hollywood was *The Naked Jungle* (1954), a Technicolor adaptation of Carl Stephenson's classic short story, "Leiningen Versus the Ants," written in 1938. George Pal, known for his excursions into the science-fiction genre, produced this taut jungle adventure thriller, which had an expertly fashioned screenplay by Philip Yordan and Ranald MacDougall, and precise, suspense-building direction from Byron Haskin. As was expected with any Pal production, the special photographic effects were superb.

The film cast Heston in the role of Christopher Leiningen, a heavy-handed man who owns a rich plantation in the upper reaches of the Amazon. ("My wife describes the character as 'one of those hero-heels you do'—and it was the first of them, and perhaps it's one of the reasons I was cast in similar roles again.") Desiring a woman to share his palatial domain, he sends for Joanna (Eleanor Parker), a mail-order bride whom he marries by proxy, but, because her matter-of-fact approach to her marital obligations conflicts with his ideas of what a wife should be, a breach develops between them. The problem nonetheless, works itself out quickly, so that the picture can concentrate on the more harrowing drama—the lethal invasion of an army of soldier ants, which destroys everything in its path.

Heston was fine as the strong, albeit desperate plantation owner who must fight to save the empire

THE NAKED JUNGLE (1954). With Eleanor Parker

SECRET OF THE INCAS (1954). With William Henry, Robert Young, and Nicole Maurey

he has taken fifteen years to build. It was not an easy role for an actor to play. One unpleasant scene, for example, required him to be smeared with syrup, then covered with ants.

His romantic interludes with Miss Parker, though not as relaxed as similar scenes he had done with Susan Hayward in *The President's Lady*, did, at any rate, contain more true feeling than audiences were used to seeing him exhibit in this sort of situation. Eleanor Parker, receiving top-billing, gave a particularly strong performance as the earthy, appealing woman who travels to a strange land to live with a man she has never met.

The Naked Jungle garnered largely favorable reviews, and, from a financial standpoint, proved to be Heston's most successful picture since *The Greatest Show on Earth*.

Immediately after completing the Pal project, Heston was set by Paramount to star in another South American-based adventure film—this one actually to be shot in Peru, rather than in Southern California. *Secret of the Incas* (original title: *Legend of the Incas*), released in May, 1954, was from an original screenplay by Ranald MacDougall and Sydney Boehm.

The mildly exciting story, which had a certain basis in fact, dealt

THE FAR HORIZONS (1955). With Fred MacMurray

with two ruthless, money-mad adventurers—Heston and Thomas Mitchell—who search for a valuable golden disc that the ancient Incas believed to have magic properties. Robert Young was an American archeologist seeking the treasure for noble reasons, while Nicole Maurey played the heroine.

Despite the freshness of its plot, some nicely etched performances by the principals, and competent direction by Jerry Hopper, the movie's strongest assets were the authentic views, in Technicolor, of the picturesque Cuzco and the Peruvian highlands as well as Macchu Picchu, the genuine lost city of antiquity, discovered in 1910. As most reviewers put it, the travelogue aspects made the picture well worth the price of admission.

Jack Moffitt, reviewing the film for *Hollywood Reporter*, complimented Heston on his contribution, then noted: "This young man has shown commendable progress since coming to Hollywood. He has yet to learn that the camera is his friend and that he does not need to act quite so hard to get over his effects. But he is doing fine. Right now, he is about mid-channel in a career that should land him among such powerful (and relaxed) giants of movie box office as Gary Cooper, Cary Grant and John Wayne. They all went through (very painfully) what he's going through now."

THE PRIVATE WAR OF MAJOR BENSON (1955).
With Tim Considine, Sal Mineo, and Butch Jones

Heston was off the screen until May of 1955, when two pictures starring the actor opened almost simultaneously. The first was the disastrous Paramount epic, *The Far Horizons*, which at various times before its release was entitled *Two Captains West, Blue Horizon, Beyond the Blue Horizon*, and *Lewis and Clark*. Scripted by Winston Miller and Edmund H. North from a novel by Della Gould Emmons, the Technicolor production purported to tell the true story of the historic Lewis and Clark expedition (1803-1806) that mapped the Louisiana Purchase and beyond. Actually, except for the most basic facts about the journey, the film was almost totally fiction—and trite fiction at that. The writers, stuck with the task of devising a feature-length entertainment about the three-year trek, apparently decided to take the easy course and fill their screenplay with a succession of well-worn episodic incidents (Indian attacks, the activities of a treacherous French guide, and the illness of Clark among them), which had no dramatic cohesion. The result was, despite director Rudolph Maté's attempts to inject some exciting action sequences, a dull, overlong film, encumbered with a fifteen-minute anti-climax back in Washington after the party returns.

Fred MacMurray received first billing as the level-headed Lewis, leader of the expedition, while Heston drew the role of the more impetuous Clark. Neither actor's performance was particularly memorable, but then they didn't have very good material to work with, either. Donna Reed won the movie's best notices as Sacajawea, the determined Shoshone Indian girl who guides the explorers to the Pacific.

Like *Secret of the Incas*, the most enjoyable element of the production was the Technicolor scenery, photographed in and around the Jackson Hole country of Wyoming.

Heston's other May, 1955 release was much more entertaining. It was his first excursion into comedy and for this actor of stern countenance to get a role in that genre, he agreed to give up his salary, in favor of a percentage of the net profits—if any. It was a wise move. The movie (negative cost: $634,000) earned nearly $4 million. "For a while," says Heston, "I was even in the hole for the restaurant lunch charges run up while we were shooting, but it all worked out fine."

The film was Universal-International's *The Private War of Major Benson*, originally developed for the talents of Cary Grant. Directed by Jerry Hopper from a screenplay by William Roberts and Richard

LUCY GALLANT (1955). With Jane Wyman

Alan Simmons, the heart-warming little saga told of how a tough, outspoken Army Major (Heston) is tamed when he is assigned to take charge of a boy's military school. Sal Mineo and Tim Hovey were among his charges and Julie Adams was his love interest.

An amusing encounter between the star and the endearing, pint-sized Master Hovey provided one of the movie's highlights. Summoned to the stern Major's office to answer charges that he had violated one of the school's minor rules, the ten-year-old announces that, because of Heston's intimidating manner, he's going to "throw up." Charlton panics. After all, he has never dealt with children before, especially sick ones. Rising from his desk in an effort to rush the lad to the nearest toilet—or, at least, to someone who can handle this situation with more expertise—he accidentally steps into the waste basket, falling flat on his face.

The movie was a charming, innocuous piece of fluff—enjoyed by the critics—which allowed Heston to prove he could take the rather hardened characters he'd been essaying and play them for comedy.

Heston hadn't appeared on television since December of 1953, when he had starred in an episode of the CBS anthology, "Medallion Theatre," entitled *A Day in Town*. However, during the final four months of 1955, he was seen in no less than four television plays—the best known of which was *Along Came Jones*, a segment of NBC's "Robert Montgomery Presents." The show was based on the Gary Cooper Western of the same name, released in 1945.

On December 29th of 1955, he did a play called *Bailout at 43,000* on CBS-TV's "Climax." This property was later sold to films and, for a time, Heston was set to repeat his assignment in the movie, working on a participation basis. However, when United Artists released the production in 1957, John Payne played the leading role.

In *Lucy Gallant*, his third 1955 release, Heston took a back seat to the film's title star, Jane Wyman, just as he had done with Jennifer Jones in *Ruby Gentry*. This Technicolor/VistaVision effort from Paramount was a typical formula woman's picture, which told how Lucy Gallant, fleeing an unhappy

romance, opens an expensive gown shop in a booming Texas oil town and builds it into one of the most successful establishments in the Southwest. Heston played the rancher who loves her, waiting in the wings until, at the end of the movie, she realizes that he is more important than her career.

The story itself wasn't anything new, having been utilized in dozens of pictures dating back to the silent era, yet the screenplay by John Lee Mahin and Winston Miller, from a novel by Margaret Cousins, contained enough clever dialogue and well-drawn characters to hold the viewer's attention for the 104-minute running time. Robert Parrish's direction moved the picture along at a lively clip, so as to camouflage somewhat the plot's familiarity. He also kept a firm, restraining hand on the players and the resulting performances by Miss Wyman, Heston, and co-stars Claire Trevor, Thelma Ritter, Wallace Ford, and William Demarest were most effective. (An added treat for the ladies, incidentally, was a fashion show, courtesy of Edith Head.)

At this point, Charlton Heston's career was still traveling on the momentum he had achieved from his association with *The Greatest Show on Earth*. He had starred in eleven pictures since then, several of which had done fairly well at the

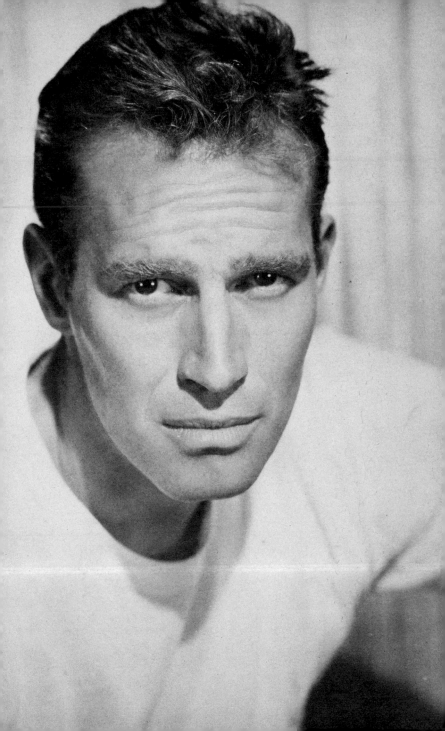

box office. However, since the majority of his films, good and bad, had failed financially, he was not considered to have much box-office pull. As a result, he seldom received offers to play the *choicest* roles available, nor could he command a *top* salary. Indeed, the only parts Heston was getting were in run-of-the-mill program efforts, made on medium or low budgets and not requiring the most stellar of names to bring in the customers.

What he needed to improve his status was another project like the circus blockbuster, and the man who gave him that second chance was the same man who had given him his first—Cecil B. DeMille.

Ever since the success of his *Samson and Delilah* in 1949, Cecil B. DeMille had wanted to remake and expand the first section of his silent classic, *The Ten Commandments*. The story of Moses and his exodus from Egypt had merely served as the prologue for a modern morality saga in the 1923 production, and the master showman now wanted to create a three- to four-hour epic —detailing the entire life of the Lawgiver—which would be his film masterpiece.

Despite the large return ($11.5 million domestic) from *Samson*, the Paramount brass was not convinced that another Biblical picture could also become a box-office winner, particularly since the *proposed* budget was $8 million. DeMille was forced to shelve his project for a while, and it remained dormant until *The Greatest Show on Earth* wound-up earning a domestic gross of $14 million for the studio. Only then did the executives acquiesce to DeMille's demands that they let him proceed with *The Ten Commandments*—a project that ultimately cost over thirteen million dollars and ran over three-and-a-half hours.

The casting of Moses was, of course, a prime consideration for the Technicolor/VistaVision spectacular, and Heston got the nod due to a lucky break—the one he had received in his nose playing college

football. This, and the fact that the producer/director liked him personally, and was also impressed with his resonant voice and rawboned resemblance to Michelangelo's statue of the prophet, were what secured for Heston this role of a lifetime.

DeMille said: "He's right for the part, not just because he resembles the Michelangelo work, but because there is a definite spiritual quality about him. He is a good man. His goodness shines through him."

Considering the lengthy preparation and the actual eight-months shooting time, the actor worked on *The Ten Commandments* for close to two years, taking a few months off when he wasn't needed to make *The Private War of Major Benson*, released well over a year before this picture.

Filming began on location in Egypt with a cast of twenty thousand extras. Heston was there for three months, while wife Lydia—pregnant with their first child—toiled in Chicago in a production of *The Seven Year Itch*.

On the set in Egypt, Heston was startled to hear semi-literate extras murmuring "Moses, Moses" as he walked by, costumed in flowing robe and beard. As a result, Heston let himself be persuaded that he

THE TEN COMMANDMENTS (1956). As Moses

must not "disillusion" the Arabs, since otherwise they might find it difficult to fall on their knees before him in the next scene. For weeks, until the sequence in question was finally shot, he never allowed himself to sit, take phone calls, drink coffee from paper cups, or behave like a relaxed human being between takes.

Those who worked on the production report that Heston truly lost himself in his role. He read and memorized whole sections of the Old Testament, studied the works of Biblical scholars, and contemplated the meaning of the Dead Sea Scrolls. Before each of his major scenes, he would go off by himself and pace back-and-forth in soli-

tary thought. On one occasion, for authenticity, he even walked barefoot across the hot, jagged rocks at the foot of Mt. Sinai.

Actor Milburn Stone, a longtime friend of Heston's, who had appeared with him in several movies, admits Heston became "ecclesiastical" while filming the mammoth production: "It's never left him. The aura's still there, all around him."

If nothing else, *The Ten Commandments* (1956) proved DeMille, even after a heart attack suffered during production, had no equal as a creator of screen spectaculars. In one panoramic scene after another, the director moved vast throngs of people before the cameras amid

THE TEN COMMANDMENTS (1956). With Yul Brynner, Sir Cedric Hardwicke, and Anne Baxter

*THE TEN COMMANDMENTS (1956). Moses brings the
Commandments to his people.*

sets of unprecedented scope. Aside from Heston, who played Moses with a forceful, carefully thought-out delineation, the stellar cast of this lavish epic included Yul Brynner as Rameses, Yvonne DeCarlo as Sephora, John Derek as Joshua, and such veteran performers as Edward G. Robinson, Vincent Price, Judith Anderson, Anne Baxter, and Nina Foch.

Fraser Heston, Heston's three-month-old son, was cast as the infant Moses in the movie. The proud father said in a post-production interview: "He's the youngest retired actor in America."

Most critics commented that the production, aside from being slowly paced and too long, suffered from DeMille's outdated melodramatic approach to the story, which, among other weaknesses, played the villains as unbelievable blackguards. Also, the parting of the Red Sea, though costing much time, effort, and money to recreate, was felt to have a theatrical, artificial look to it. The adverse criticisms, at any rate, seemed to make no difference when it came to box-office returns because *The Ten Commandments* garnered a domestic gross of $43 million.

Surprisingly, Heston didn't benefit immediately from the success of the DeMille epic. The more prestigious roles he sought did not come to him for another three years.

THREE VIOLENT PEOPLE (1957).
With Anne Baxter and Tom Tryon

On December 5, 1956, the actor opened in New York at the City Center in a 'revival of the Joshua Logan/Thomas Heggen World War II comedy, *Mister Roberts*, staged by John Forsythe. Of his re-creation of the role originally played by Henry Fonda, the *New York World-Telegram and Sun* said: "Charlton Heston plays the title character with warmth and a kind of muscular intensity that is perhaps a touch solemn, but, nevertheless, fills the bill nicely."

To capitalize on what they hoped would be a new surge of popularity for their contract star, Paramount had, right after the DeMille film was completed, rushed Heston into a moderately interesting Western, which was released two months after *Commandments*, in early 1957. *Three Violent People* (original title: *The Mavericks*) co-starred Anne Baxter, Gilbert Roland, Forrest Tucker, and Tom Tryon in a bitter-tinged but romantic yarn about the carpetbaggers who tried to take over the Southwest in 1866. James Edward Grant wrote the screenplay, which was directed by Rudolph Maté.

Heston's character was another hero/heel—akin to what he had played in *The Naked Jungle*. He was a Confederate, returning to his ranch after the Civil War to discover that he must fight a crooked political machine in order to keep his land and his cattle. Miss Baxter played his feisty bride, whom he married on impulse.

The movie was a passable programmer, but, certainly not one that would be long remembered after viewers left the theater. Most disappointing was the climactic confrontation between Heston's forces and the heavies. One got the impression that the sequence, quite abrupt in its execution, was sluffed-off because the production was behind schedule and the director had to make the time up somewhere.

Heston refused the top role in Warner Brothers' World War II film, *Darby's Rangers* (1958), ultimately played by James Garner, and, instead, decided to do some more television, appearing on four dramatic shows in the years 1957-58. The most notable production was a "Playhouse 90" adaptation of John P. Marquand's *Point of No Return* (February 20, 1958), in which he co-starred with Hope Lange.

There is hardly an actor in Hollywood who would not jump at the chance to be directed in a picture by Orson Welles, the creative genius of *Citizen Kane*. The actor-director had been living in European self-exile for a few years, when producer Albert Zugsmith signed him to appear in an unimportant programmer from Universal, *Man in the Shadow*. A good working rela-

THREE VIOLENT PEOPLE (1957). With Anne Baxter

TOUCH OF EVIL (1958). With Orson Welles

tionship developed between the men and, as a result, Zugsmith set Welles to both write and appear in his next project, *Touch of Evil* (1958), based on a novel by Whit Masterson, called *Badge of Evil*.

Heston was the next star signed for the film, agreeing to play the story's hero only because he had assumed that Welles would be directing. Learning of Heston's motivation, Zugsmith quickly set Welles for that job as well.

Shot on a low budget which required the filmmakers to use sections of Venice, California, as a substitute for the movie's actual locale of a Mexican border town, the picture presented Welles as Hank Quinlan, a corrupt cop, who always gets his man—even if he has to plant phony evidence. Quinlan runs into problems after he frames Janet Leigh, the newlywed American wife of Heston, for a crime he committed himself—the murder of dope smuggler Akim Tamiroff. Heston, an official with the Mexican government, goes after the fat man to prove his wife's innocence. The movie ends with Quinlan being killed by his own aide.

As always, Welles turned out a fascinating, atmospheric picture, containing an unusual story, hard-hitting dialogue, effective low-key lighting, and, above all, his own bravura performance as the gro-

tesque villain. Reviewers praised him for his directorial style and innovative touches, but they were forced to admit that, as an entity, *Touch of Evil* was often incoherent and, in many instances, had its colorful characters acting without adequate motivation.

The problem, however, was not really Welles' fault, as Zugsmith recalls: "The studio felt that Welles was being 'difficult' in the way he wanted to cut the film. Actually, Orson is anything but 'difficult' to work with—*if* you understand the man. He always had a good reason for what he wanted—even if that reason was not apparent to the casual eye.

"What he really needed was a buffer between himself and the Universal front office, but while the movie was being edited, I, regrettably, was over at MGM preparing another project, so Orson had to deal with the head editor—a man with old-fashioned ideas—and the publicity chief himself. He knocked heads with both and, as a result, was taken off the picture.

"Harry Keller came in and directed a couple of additional scenes with Heston, which the studio felt would explain the story better. The final cut—minus many of the original scenes—was, of course, nothing like Orson had intended, and it, frankly, altered the entire pacing of the picture."

TOUCH OF EVIL (1958). With Janet Leigh

THE BIG COUNTRY (1958). As Steve Leech

THE BIG COUNTRY (1958). With Gregory Peck

Touch of Evil was neither a "prestige" movie, nor one of exploitation caliber, which meant that the studio really didn't know how to sell it to the public. It was sluffed-off, and except for the more astute viewers who recognized Welles' brilliance, passed unnoticed through its release dates. Happily, the film became a favorite with Welles cultists and, in recent years, has been seen frequently in the director's retrospectives. In his book *The Great Movies*, William Bayer calls it "perhaps the greatest 'B' movie ever made."

Extensively made-up, Heston turned in an adequate, off-beat portrayal in the secondary, though top-billed role of the Mexican official. For him, the important factor was not the part but working with the director: "Welles is one of the few authentic talents in the business—and he gets better every year."

His desire to work with only the finest of directors was the prime inducement for Heston's accepting a decidedly supporting role in his next film, *The Big Country* (1958), a lengthy, wide-screen Western by William Wyler. Billed fourth in a cast which included Gregory Peck, Jean Simmons, Carroll Baker, Burl Ives (who won the Oscar for Best Supporting Actor), Charles Bickford, and Chuck Connors, Heston

THE BUCCANEER (1958). As Andrew Jackson, leading the battle

played Steve Leech, the rugged ranch foreman for Major Henry Terrill (Bickford). The Major is engaged in a bitter range feud with Rufus Hannassey (Ives), a neighbor. Into this tense situation comes easterner James McKay (Peck), planning to marry Terrill's spoiled daughter (Miss Baker). Through his efforts and those of Julie Maragon (Miss Simmons), the dispute is finally settled when the two clan leaders meet to fight matters out between themselves.

The film was shot in color near Stockton, California, from a screenplay based on a novel by Donald Hamilton. Heston certainly did not have a pivotal role in the drama and, except for picking a fight with hero Peck and making a pass at Miss Baker, really initiated none of the story's important action. In this comparatively bland assignment, he spent most of his time merely standing around or riding off to carry out Bickford's orders. There was no doubt that he contributed a sturdy performance but then, the part was not too dissimilar from some he had done a few years earlier at Paramount.

For a movie that started filming without a completed screenplay, this sweeping $3-million entertainment turned out to be surprisingly good, even though reviews were mixed. Well-rounded characters in

BEN-HUR (1959). With Stephen Boyd

BEN-HUR (1959). With Cathy O'Donnell, Martha Scott, and Haya Harareet

a story that continually held viewer interest, deft performances by a top-flight cast, a rich score by Jerome Moross serving as background to some breathtaking scenery, and the masterful direction of William Wyler, were among the elements that made *The Big Country* one of the best Westerns of its day.

Under his original contract, Heston still owed Paramount one more picture. He satisfied that commitment by requesting a role in what would be Cecil B. DeMille's final film, a six-million-dollar remake of his *The Buccaneer*, which had starred Fredric March in the 1938 version. In this 1958 release, Heston would play General Andrew Jackson, reprising the part he had essayed in *The President's Lady*—with Yul Brynner in the lead role of pirate Jean Lafitte. (*Time:* "*The Buccaneer* introduces to the moviegoing millions the most exciting new film personality since Clark Gable with a mustache: Yul Brynner with hair.")

Seventy-seven-year-old DeMille, in reality, merely served as executive producer on this production, which, in very wordy fashion, told how Lafitte turned patriot and won pardon for his men by aiding Jackson at the Battle of New Orleans.

BEN-HUR (1959). The chariot race

The actual producer was onetime star Henry Wilcoxon, while the showman's son-in-law, actor Anthony Quinn, assumed the directorial reins.

The result, said to have been cut by DeMille himself, was a stagnant period piece, containing little more than some exquisite sets and costumes. Performances from a talented cast, including Charles Boyer, Claire Bloom, and Inger Stevens, seemed uninspired, and the few action sequences were rather dull. As Jackson, Heston interpreted the role with a bit more flamboyancy than he had enlisted in 1953. It was one of his less notable portrayals.

Though *The Ten Commandments* had not significantly altered Heston's Hollywood status as the strong, taciturn hero of program pictures, it did renew the momentum he had achieved from *The Greatest Show on Earth* and did keep him working. The film that *would* give him the career boost he had been waiting for, and, also, forever solidify his position in the industry as a *major* star, was the 1959 spectacular, *Ben-Hur*.

Metro-Goldwyn-Mayer, in bad financial trouble, was gambling that this $14-million remake (at that time, the most expensive movie ever produced) of the 1925 silent classic would make the studio sol-

THE WRECK OF THE MARY DEARE (1959). With Gary Cooper

vent again. To insure the quality of the huge undertaking, William Wyler was signed to direct and Karl Tunberg was set to adapt Lew Wallace's religious novel about Christ. (Later, Christopher Fry also worked on the screenplay, but was denied credit by the Writers Guild.)

There had been some talk about casting Cesare Danova in the movie's title role, but Wyler, remembering the good relationship he'd shared with Heston on *The Big Country*, insisted that he be given the choice assignment. The actor was still working on *The Buccaneer* when he signed the contract that would relocate him and his family to Rome for the project's nine-month shooting schedule, then return him to Hollywood for an additional two months of work. Indeed, the movie came along at a very inconvenient time for Heston, since he had just begun construction on a mountain-top home above Beverly Hills and was forced to leave while the house was completed without his personal supervision. (He would finally move into the dwelling during the early part of 1960.)

In a film as vast in scope as *Ben-Hur*, actors often get lost in the spectacle. Not so with a Wyler picture, as Heston explained to writer Pete Martin in a 1960 interview with the *Saturday Evening Post*:

"Willie Wyler makes his pictures with the idea of keeping the people in them the important thing. While he'd never made a movie as colossal as *Ben-Hur*, he set out to make that intimate, too. Willie says it's the toughest picture he's ever made . . .

"How could Willie make the story of Ben-Hur memorable because of what happened to the individual characters, when it included a battle between two fleets of sea galleys, a race with nine four-horse chariots, eight-thousand yowling extras as spectators, and, at the end of the picture, tossed in as an extra spectacle, the crucifixion of Christ? If Willie succeeded—and some people feel that he did—he brought off Hollywood's first intimate spectacle."*

The most exciting sequence in the production was, of course, the chariot race between Judah Ben-Hur and his arch-enemy, Messala, the Roman officer who had imprisoned his onetime friend's mother and sister, then sent him into slavery on the galleys. Shot over a three-month period by second-unit directors Yakima Canutt and Andrew Marton, this sensational contest would become the highlight of the picture and, more than any other factor, be responsible for its ultimate world-

*Pete Martin, "I Call on Ben-Hur," *Saturday Evening Post*, August 20, 1960, p. 40.

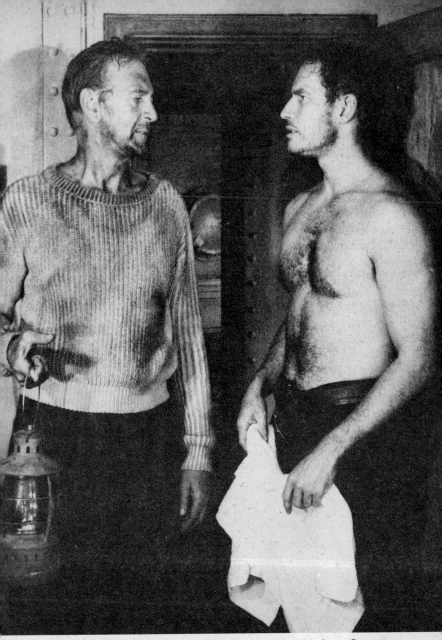

THE WRECK OF THE MARY DEARE (1959). With Gary Cooper

wide gross of $65 million. For his part in these scenes, Heston worked six weeks learning how to manage a chariot and four white horses. "Nearly pulled my arms right out of their sockets," he says.

Another strong episode was the star's imprisonment as a galley slave, particularly the scene in which he first meets Roman tribune Jack Hawkins who, sensing he is dealing with an extraordinarily proud prisoner, tests his will by the sting of the whip.

The literate screenplay and Wyler's sensitive, well-formulated direction in both inspirational scenes, such as the Crucifixion, and those of thundering action, such as the sea battle, combined to make *Ben-Hur* a splendid piece of entertainment and one of the most intelligent epics of all time.

As the unjustly enslaved Jew seeking revenge, Heston contributed a multi-dimensional performance which elicited favorable reviews from the world press. The supporting players—Stephen Boyd (Messala), Jack Hawkins, Hugh Griffith, and Haya Harareet—also contributed fascinating in-depth characterizations.

Upon completing his work for Wyler, Heston decided that, as a change of pace, he should do a picture with a modern setting, and therefore signed to co-star with an ill and aging Gary Cooper in MGM's *The Wreck of the Mary Deare* (1959), based on the Hammond Innes suspense novel which, in turn, had been inspired by the real-life enigma of the ghost ship *Mary Celeste*.

Directed by Michael Anderson from Eric Ambler's screenplay, the film, shot in England, tells how salvage boat skipper Heston becomes involved with the mystery freighter *Mary Deare*, which, while floundering, had nearly rammmed his craft in a stormy sea. He boards the vessel and finds it abandoned, except for the baffling captain (Cooper) who proceeds to scuttle the ship on the rock-infested Minkies. After hearing Cooper's explanation for his strange actions, Heston agrees to help expose the saga's true villains. Then, following a London court inquiry into the mishap, the stars embark on a dangerous underwater mission inside the hull of the *Mary Deare* to retrieve evidence to exonerate the captain.

Both stars were perfectly cast in this smartly directed, skillfully photographed adventure yarn —particularly Cooper, who, in the central role, conveyed a surprising range of emotion and reaction considering the taciturn image projected in most of his previous pictures. Sadly, the illness that would soon take his life was quite apparent in many scenes as well.

THE WRECK OF THE MARY DEARE (1959). As John Sands

Heston, though effective in his assignment, actually had a thankless part, which, despite its substantial size, gave him little to do except react to Cooper or stand around looking concerned. An actor who always insists upon doing his own stunts, Heston learned to salvage dive for the movie's climactic scenes: "I was forbidden to go any deeper than forty feet. When I reached one hundred feet, I knew I had it licked."

The Wreck of the Mary Deare made its debut around the country almost simultaneously with *Ben-Hur*, but, because of a script which slowed considerably during the middle of the action, reviews were only fair and the picture created little excitement with the public.

Heston elected to do some summer theater in 1959 ("to renew my passport"), choosing to star in *Macbeth* at the University of Michigan's Drama Festival at Ann Arbor, then in *State of the Union*, with wife Lydia, at the Santa Barbara Summer Theatre.

Back in Los Angeles, he gave an interview to *Variety* in which he stated that the then current trend of actors entering independent film production was not for him: "Lots of actors make a mistake on independent production. They leap into vehicles just because they think they will make themselves a million dollars. But I didn't come into this profession to get rich. I was an actor before I was a star, and I am an actor still."

He proved his point by refusing the co-starring role opposite Marilyn Monroe in Fox's *Let's Make Love* (Yves Montand played it) in favor of returning to Broadway to be directed by his idol, Laurence Olivier, in Benn W. Levy's play, *The Tumbler*, which opened at the Helen Hayes Theatre on February 24, 1960. Panned by the critics, this dull story of a sex triangle in rural England played a mere five performances. Rosemary Harris, Martha Scott, and Donald Moffat appeared with Heston, of whom Richard Watts Jr. of the *New York Post* said: "Mr. Heston, who is clearly a serious and intelligent actor, is hopelessly bogged down in the prolixity of what I take to be the title role."

Reflecting on the experience, Heston would later say: "I feel I'm the only one who came out of it with a profit. The producers lost money, the writer lost months of work, Larry Olivier lost out, too. But I got out of it precisely what I went in for—a chance to work with Olivier. I learned from him in six weeks things I never would have learned otherwise. I think I ended up a better actor, with more responsibility."

Nobody in Hollywood was really

Holding his Oscar for BEN-HUR

surprised when on Oscar night in April, 1960, *Ben-Hur* won eleven of the gold statuettes—more than any other film in history. Among these honors were Best Picture, Best Director, Best Actor (Heston), Best Supporting Actor (Hugh Griffith), and Best Music Score (Miklos Rozsa).

Only the announcement of Heston's win caused anybody to raise an eyebrow. Not that the audience was disappointed that this popular member of their industry had captured the coveted prize, but most felt that, with both James Stewart (*Anatomy of a Murder*) and Paul Muni (*The Last Angry Man*) in the running, nobody else had much of a chance. Wags would later theorize that Heston rode in on the coattails of the prize-winning spectacular.

On receiving his trophy from presenter Susan Hayward, Heston made a short acceptance speech to the audience, in which he said, "Thank you, Christopher Fry," acknowledging the contribution of the script's uncredited writer. This off-hand remark infuriated the Writers Guild of America—of which Fry was not a member—and resulted in the organization's writing the star a harsh letter in which they described his comment as "reprehensible and damaging."

Replying to the Guild, Heston said, in part: "It never occurred to me to get clearance from your organization for my expression of gratitude. . . . Is it your intention to expunge Mr. Fry's name from the lips of men?"

(Interestingly, writer Karl Tunberg was the only artist nominated for *Ben-Hur* who did not win in his respective category.)

Now, in the spring of 1960, Charlton Heston had not only headlined two of Hollywood's most successful motion pictures, but had also won an Academy Award for his mantle. Offers for other *important* projects began to come his way . . . and not surprisingly, many of these films were of a particular genre.

It's been said that a performer never achieves true stardom until he's typed. John Wayne is identified with Westerns; Cary Grant excels at sophisticated comedy; and, once he had won his Oscar, Charlton Heston *seemed* to do one spectacular costume drama after another. Actually, he appeared in a wide variety of film roles following *Ben-Hur*, but it is the memory of the sweeping epics—biblical, medieval, and otherwise—which has remained most vivid with the public.

Perhaps the best of these post-Oscar period pieces was *El Cid* (1961), in which he co-starred with Sophia Loren. It was produced in Spain on a budget of $7 million by Samuel Bronston—the man who had discovered how cheaply "casts of thousands" could be hired in that country—and released in 70 mm-Super Technirama/Technicolor by Allied Artists. Anthony Mann directed this moving tale about Rodrigo Diaz (1040?-1099), one of Spain's greatest heroes.

Known as "The Cid" (meaning "the lord"), Diaz had served in the army of Sancho II of Castile, but after the murder of the monarch by his brother Alfonso, he was banished. From that point, The Cid formed his own army and, in 1094, conquered Valencia from the Moors.

The screenplay by Fredric M.

A HEAP OF EPICS

Frank and Phil Yordan was engrossing, containing varied episodes of court intrigue, an unusual romance featuring a love/hate relationship between the principals, interesting though superficial characters such as Genevieve Page's scheming princess, and much action. Crammed with pageantry that made it a kind of pictorially affluent Spanish *Ivanhoe*, *El Cid* moved along at a smart pace, taking every opportunity to display the landscapes of scenic Spain. Indeed, the views of Valencia were magnificent.

With Miklos Rozsa contributing one of his better scores, and Yakima Canutt staging the vast battle sequences, the film delighted audiences and earned a domestic gross of $12 million.

In the title role of the conscience-stricken warrior, who in the early scenes of the picture must prove that an act of mercy on his part is not a betrayal of his king, Heston was very convincing—his stilted qualities giving the character a proper dignity. Miss Loren's role as his wife, on the other hand, was not too challenging, yet she brought a warmth to the part which made it come to life. Regrettably, as was often the case with Heston, his love scenes with the actress were somewhat awkward.

EL CID (1961). With Sophia Loren

Much better was the sequence in which he forces the weak Alfonso (John Fraser) to swear before a large gathering of his subjects that *he* is not responsible for his brother Sancho's murder. The newly crowned king takes the oath reluctantly, then, resenting Diaz' disrespectful act, orders his banishment.

Heston played the confrontation with a vengeance, making it, from a strictly dramatic standpoint, the most memorable scene in the picture.

"I like portraying heroes of antiquity whose values were grander and more spectacular than those of today," Heston admitted to an interviewer during *El Cid*'s eight-month shooting schedule. "Not every star can do this convincingly. I do not mean this as a judgment of anyone's acting ability, but can you picture Cary Grant in a toga, or Elvis Presley in a suit of armor? It would be a complete contradiction of the public images they have worked so hard to establish. . . . I have to admit that wearing costumes always has appealed to the ham in me."

When the movie opened at the Warner Theatre in New York, an illuminated 600-square foot billboard overlooking Times Square announced the fact—with both stars' names appearing in equal size. Because of the vertical nature of the sign, however, Miss Loren's name appeared below Heston's,

EL CID (1961). In the title role

prompting the Italian actress to file suit against Bronston Productions, charging a grievous breach of contract. Her complaint read, in part: "If the defendants are permitted to place deponent's name below that of Charlton Heston, then it will appear that deponent's status is considered to be inferior to that of Charlton Heston. ... It is impossible to determine or even to estimate the extent of the damages which the plaintiff will suffer."

Miss Loren lost the suit.

Back from Spain, Heston was visiting Oklahoma City in May of 1961 as a house guest of the head of the University of Oklahoma Medical School, when he announced to the press that he would participate in a demonstration protesting segregation policies at some of the city's eating establishments. "When I found out what was going on," he explained, "I wanted to stand up and be counted."

He spoke up again in December, this time in his position as vice president of the Screen Actors' Guild (SAG). Addressing Congress, he called for changes in the U.S. tax laws to discourage film production overseas by American companies, and the consideration of a subsidy, financed out of theater admission taxes, for moviemaking in this country.

"I'm fortunate," he told reporters. "I make more than a liv-ing. The time I might have spent doing something else, that's the time I use to help others. Seems to me I shouldn't spend all that time playing tennis. Seems to me I should put something back in."

Late in 1961, Charlton and Lydia Heston adopted an infant girl, naming her Holly Ann.

Two Heston pictures went into release during 1962, neither of them very notable. The first was a whacky little comedy from Paramount, *The Pigeon That Took Rome*, written, produced, and directed by Melville Shavelson and derived from a novel, *The Easter Dinner*, by Donald Downes. Heston, in an amusing change-of-pace, played an American infantry officer assigned to an espionage mission in Nazi-occupied Rome (where the picture was shot), only to learn that his sole contact with the Yank forces, homing pigeons, have been serving as meals for an unknowing Italian family. German birds are enlisted as replacements, resulting in a comedy of errors. Elsa Martinelli, Harry Guardino, and Brian Donlevy also appeared in this light but diverting comedy, yet the movie did nothing at the box office.

Diamond Head, from Columbia, proved more commercial than the Paramount release, but, sadly, did not approach it in artistic merit. Based on a lengthy, popular novel

*On television with Fred Astaire
in THE FUGITIVE EYE (1961)*

THE PIGEON THAT TOOK ROME (1962). As Capt. Paul MacDougall

by Peter Gilman, the film adaptation by Marguerite Roberts failed in that it attempted to tackle the story's emotional and social issues—implied incest and racial prejudice—by employing much too superficial an approach. Heston, as a wealthy Hawaiian landowner who opposes the marriage of his sister (Yvette Mimieux) to a pure-blooded Island youth, gave strength to his ill-conceived part, which, at the film's end, had the star suddenly—without sufficient motivation—turning magnanimous after 100 minutes of acting the heel. Guy Green's staid direction was barely adequate, which is more than can be said for either Sam Leavitt's cinematography, which managed to make the Hawaiian scenery look rather dull, or the supporting performances.

His only theatrical release of 1963 was another Spanish-filmed Samuel Bronston/Allied Artists epic, *55 Days at Peking*, which dealt with the Chinese Boxer Rebellion of 1900. Budgeted at approximately $6 million, the breathtakingly photographed production starred, along with Heston, Ava Gardner, David Niven, John Ireland, and Paul Lukas. Nicholas Ray directed from a script by Bernard Gordon and Philip Yordan.

Peking related a potentially fascinating tale of how nationals from many countries usually in opposition were trapped in the international compound and besieged by hordes of rebellious Chinese. As Mr. Bronston explained: "The unity of peoples, no matter what their beliefs, in the face of danger! This incident is what the United Nations symbolizes but has not yet achieved."

Regrettably, the 2½ hour spectacular, though well paced with many skillfully staged action sequences, was handicapped by a host of stereotyped characters moving through some trite dramatic confrontations. Niven was stalwart as the British ambassador who forces the other nations to remain firm in their stand against the Boxers, but Miss Gardner as a Russian baroness with a questionable past seemed very indifferent to what was going on around her. Flora Robson as the despotic Empress of China was appropriately regal but also stolid.

Heston, who did the movie as a special favor to Phil Yordan, considered it one of his most miserable filmmaking experiences, due to the fact that the screenplay was incomplete when shooting began, and also because he found his leading lady undisciplined. For his role as an American Marine major, he ably re-employed his now-familiar hero/heel characterization.

Like *The Private War of Major Benson*, Heston had another affect-

87

DIAMOND HEAD (1962). With George Chakiris and Yvette Mimieux

55 DAYS AT PEKING (1963). As Major Matt Lewis

ing relationship with a child in this film. Adorable Lynne Sue Moon played the half-Chinese daughter of one of the major's fellow officers (Jerome Thor), who is killed in an early battle. The major doesn't really want to be encumbered with this orphan, but with Sergeant John Ireland serving as his uninvited conscience, he takes her along with him at the film's conclusion.

Colorful costumes, lavish settings, and a stirring score by Dimitri Tiomkin were the main assets of the picture, which garnered a domestic gross of $5 million. (One amusing production problem Bronston faced was finding sufficient Oriental extras for the movie's vast crowd scenes. He discovered early that a mere handful of Chinese lived in Spain, so 1500 Orientals were imported from various countries to be in the picture.)

On November 15, 1963, Heston was seen as Thomas Jefferson in the "Hallmark Hall of Fame" production of *The Patriots*, airing over NBC-TV. George Schaefer directed.

Heston was off the screen completely in 1964, but, the following year, he appeared in four pictures—all of which received a fair share of publicity, but none that really enhanced his career. George Stevens' religious drama, *The Greatest Story Ever Told* (1965),

was the first released. Loosely basing his picture on Fulton Oursler's best-selling book about Christ, Stevens intended to create a definitive biography, "a Biblical classic that has vigor in ideas—with no souped-up spectacles, no sword fights, no bacchanalian orgies."

"Stevens took forever to shoot this," recalls actor Michael Ansara, who played one of the project's many cameo roles. "Time and money meant nothing, because he thought he was making the greatest epic of all time—his masterpiece.

"Some days he would take several hours to set up a shot, then decide to abandon it altogether. We averaged one or two set-ups a day—and, on a few occasions, nothing was filmed at all."

Over budget (by $10 million) and overlong (225 minutes, which was later cut down to 141), the film opened amid great fanfare and was thoroughly panned by the critics. Most agreed that the Utah locales and Stevens' stately religious tableaux were beautiful to behold, but a pretty picture does not a movie make, and the verdict from both reviewers and the public was that, despite all good intentions, *The Greatest Story Ever Told* was boredom incarnate—a self-indulgent, lethargically paced work by one of the screen's greatest artists.

THE GREATEST STORY EVER TOLD (1965). As John the Baptist

Also criticized was the fact that Stevens had used stars—many of whom were totally out-of-place—for virtually every speaking role. Probably the most ludicrous piece of casting was John Wayne as the centurion who leads Christ (played like a waxworks figure by Max von Sydow) to the Cross. The "Duke" reads his sole line with much "awh," in a scene that seemed to go on for thirty minutes.

Joining such performers as Sidney Poitier, Carroll Baker, José Ferrer, Telly Savalas, Claude Rains, Sal Mineo, and Ed Wynn in the "Spot the Star" game, Heston played John the Baptist with much grit and gusto—reminiscent of his Moses in *The Ten Commandments*.

Concurrent with the release of his next picture in March of 1965, Heston was awarded the Silver Medallion of Brotherhood from the National Conference of Christians and Jews.

The film that opened that month was Columbia's Civil War Western, *Major Dundee*, which had made news several months earlier when Heston, in an unprecedented move, gave up his salary of $200,-000 for the privilege of sticking to the movie's original script by Harry Julian Fink, Oscar Saul, and the project's controversial director, Sam Peckinpah.

Dundee told of a troop of U. S. Cavalry—aided by Confederate prisoners-of-war—chasing a mur-

MAJOR DUNDEE (1965). In the title role

MAJOR DUNDEE (1965). With Senta Berger

derous Apache and his band into Mexico to rescue three kidnapped white children and avenge an Indian massacre. Shot in Mexico, the production began going well beyond its original schedule and cost, prompting the studio heads to demand that the screenplay be revised so that two key character-developing scenes be combined and filmed back in Hollywood.

Both Heston and Peckinpah objected to the change, arguing that it would damage the movie artistically. The studio, not wanting to abandon their investment, had no choice but to go along with the men and the scenes were shot as originally written.

Back home, however, Heston, who had always been opposed to actors who caused problems on sets, decided that his position with Columbia—though artistically justified—was, nevertheless, questionable. Therefore, through his agent, he offered to return his entire fee for the film. At first, the studio bigwigs said that they could not think of accepting, but, a few days later—to Heston's surprise—they called back, stating they had changed their minds and would take the money. When asked later by the press if his gesture might establish a trend with fellow performers, Heston replied: "Trend, hell! It isn't establishing any trend with me!"

Unfortunately, Heston's

THE AGONY AND THE ECSTASY (1965). As Michelangelo

THE AGONY AND THE ECSTASY (1965). With Rex Harrison

"supreme" sacrifice was for naught, since the scenes in question were ultimately excluded from the finished picture, resulting in a disturbingly unexplained change in the star's character near the finish. Perhaps if Peckinpah had been allowed control over the editing of his film, there would have been a decidedly different result, rather than the episodic tedium audiences experienced.

On the plus side, the director did stage several taut, well-played scenes, and the actors—Heston, Richard Harris, James Coburn, and Brock Peters—delivered solid performances. These assets, however, were not strong enough to overcome the often incoherent nature of the production.

In September, moviegoers were able to view Heston's interpretation of Michelangelo in Fox's adaptation of Irving Stone's novel, *The Agony and the Ecstasy*. Stone's biography of the sculptor-painter dealt with his entire life, but the dramatization was limited to Michelangelo's painting of the ceiling of the Sistine Chapel, as well as the personal confict he continually experienced with his patron, Pope Julius II, brilliantly played by Rex Harrison. Carol Reed served as director on the project, scripted by Philip Dunne.

In preparing for his role, Heston viewed as many of the artist's works as possible, read scores of books and papers on the subject, studied techniques of sculpture and fresco painting, and attempted to match, as closely as possible, his appearance to Michelangelo's. A thinned face, short hair and beard, and a plastic noodle jammed into his nose to push it out of joint created an excellent resemblance.

Heston tried hard to make this portrayal viable, but, unfortunately, what ended up on the screen was a characterization with seemingly little depth. He projected the artist's pride well, but one found it difficult to believe that this grimacing man had the sensitivity to create the great masterpieces Michelangelo is responsible for. Truly, it was the worst miscasting of the actor's career.

Of course, to be fair, it must be admitted that Dunne's screenplay also left much to be desired. One scene which drew unexpected audience laughter was that in which the artist gained his inspiration for what he would etch on the chapel's ceiling. Sitting on a mountain top, he watches the clouds as they form what he will eventually paint. This dramatic moment teetered on the edge of absurdity, but, like the rest of the film, it was helped by Alex North's moving score. The Rome-based production's most impressive feature was, undoubtedly, its remarkable settings, which included a re-creation of the Sistine Chapel—enhanced by the exquisite

THE WAR LORD (1965). With Rosemary Forsyth and Guy Stockwell

THE WAR LORD (1965). With Rosemary Forsyth

camera work of Leon Shamroy.

Undemanding viewers found *The Agony and the Ecstasy* to be entertaining, although most critics called it trite and dull. Evidently, this was the prevailing opinion since its domestic gross was only $4 million.

Heston had wanted to do a film version of Leslie Stevens' unsuccessful Broadway play, *The Lovers*, for four years. He finally got it before the cameras in October, 1964, as a joint production of his newly formed Court Productions and Universal Pictures. Set in eleventh-century Belgium, *The War Lord* (1965), as the movie was finally called, was another of the performer's films that suffered because the director, Franklin Schaffner, and the studio had different ideas as to the handling of the story material.

Millard Kaufman and John Collier's screenplay told of a knight (Heston) who falls heir to a small Norman fief on the coast of the North Sea. Invoking the ancient *droit du seigneur* whereby a nobleman may claim the virginity of a bride on her wedding night, he brings a beautiful peasant girl (Rosemary Forsyth, instead of first choice Julie Christie) to his castle, and as a result incurs the wrath of the villagers.

"John Collier, Franklin Schaffner and myself planned it as a simple love story," Heston said to interviewers, "contrasted with an examination of witchcraft rituals of the Middle Ages. But Universal saw it differently—as a minor league *El Cid*.

"Most of the witchcraft material wound up on the cutting room floor, and, with the studio insisting the climactic siege be built up, the story's intimacy was ruined."

The production was not an expensive one, since, rather than going on location to France, the company opted to build a Medieval village and tower on the Universal back lot at a cost of $250,000.

Slowly paced, bewildering in its final structure, and peppered with such inspired lines as "I hate your knightly guts," *The War Lord* did poorly at the box office. Some observers claimed it had an interesting story, aided by competent performances, but was simply too cerebral for popular taste.

In 1965, Heston was first elected President of Screen Actors' Guild, serving in that capacity subsequently for a total of six terms. He also returned to the stage and appeared with wife Lydia in a production of Robert Bolt's drama about Sir Thomas More, *A Man For All Seasons*, which played the Mill Run Playhouse in Chicago, then later, in Stokie, Illinois. In March of 1966, he performed the play in the Greater Los Angeles area at the Valley Music Theatre.

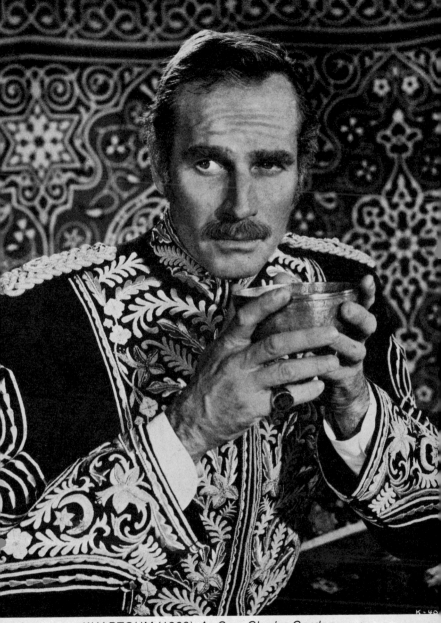

KHARTOUM (1966). As Gen. Charles Gordon

KHARTOUM (1966). Gen. Gordon is attacked by the Sudanese.

Of his portrayal in the latter production, Cecil Smith of the *Los Angeles Times* said: "Heston's performance is magnificent, rooted in lush soil. He has caught not only the grandeur that was More and the saintliness and passion, but the guts of the man."

Heston continued to travel around the globe on a regular basis—to visit troops in Vietnam, do readings in Nigeria for the State Department, and also make movies. Thus, his only 1966 release was filmed in England and Egypt.

United Artists' epic film, *Khartoum*, told the true story of British General Charles "Chinese" Gordon, who, in 1885, traveled to the city of Khartoum in the Sudan to defend it from the Arab hordes of a fanatical religious leader known as the Mahdi. After a 317-day siege, the fortress, devoid of supplies and ammunition, fell to the Mahdi's dervishes and Gordon, one of Britain's greatest heroes, was killed.

Directed by Basil Dearden, the lavish movie was moderately entertaining but hampered by Robert Ardrey's wordy screenplay which did not develop its principal roles past the two-dimensional plateau. Nevertheless, with actors like Laurence Olivier playing the Mahdi and Ralph Richardson playing Prime Minister Gladstone, the characters were endowed with qualities not inherent in the original material.

Heston had a fine grasp on the character of the arrogant, very-English Gordon—a mystic, who, in his final scene, when confronted by the mob of Arabs storming his quarters, momentarily holds them at bay with his hypnotic gaze. It was a quiet role, but one that radiated great strength.

The three months of careful research into Gordon's background was certainly worthwhile for the actor, since the picture contains one of his best screen performances.

Expertly staged battle sequences featuring thousands of extras, a lush score by Frank Cordell, and a series of overwhelming panoramas of the Sudan were positive factors in this historical saga, which did little business in theaters. It was unfortunate, because the movie's assets definitely outweighed its script deficiencies.

His last few films having failed, it was apparent that Heston's name on a marquee gave no assurance that an expensive costume picture would earn a hefty financial return. His continued participation in this type of project had, in fact, made him fair game for nightclub and television comics. Perhaps a change in the kind of roles he was playing was in order.

"I'm grateful," Heston told a *Coronet* interviewer, "very grateful I had the chance to play such roles as Moses, John the Baptist, Ben-Hur, Michelangelo, and the others but, well, enough is enough. Besides, I want to concentrate on films that depict current situations, deal with current social themes. Remember, film is the most effective means of communicating ideas ever devised by the hand of man. I want to do films that get across our ideas, the ideas of this country. Believe me, there is no better flag-carrier to the far corners of the world than the American film. And I want to be, must be, a part of that flag-carrying."

In an effort to divorce himself from the larger-than-life epic roles he'd become identified with, Heston signed to star in *Counterpoint* (original title: *The Battle Horns*), a tense World War II melodrama from Universal. Released in 1967, this thriller cast the star in the unlikely role of a conductor of an American symphony orchestra, who, while on a U. S. O. tour in Belgium, is taken captive with his musicians during the Battle of the Bulge. The German commander, a music lover, temporarily overlooks his orders to shoot all prisoners, provided that the conductor treats him to a special performance.

Heston, though occasionally

IT'S NICE TO WORK REGULAR

overplaying his part, was adequate as the musical genius who must see that his people escape the Nazis' wrath, and Maximilian Schell gave a strong performance as his German nemesis in what evolved into a battle of wits between the two men. Based on Alan Sillitoe's novel, *The General*, James Lee and Joel Oliansky's screenplay included some contrived incidents and poorly developed characters, which, despite the fast pacing maintained by director Ralph Nelson, resulted in the production's failure to rise above programmer status.

About the time he was shooting *Counterpoint*, Heston was asked to follow in the footsteps of former actors George Murphy and Ronald Reagan and run for public office. His reply was quite firm: "Absolutely *not*! I've played three Presidents (Jackson, Jefferson, and, in a television documentary, the voice of F. D. R.), two saints, and two geniuses and that's enough for me."

On January 31, 1968, Charlton was seen as Essex in the "Hallmark Hall of Fame" production of *Elizabeth the Queen*, airing over NBC-TV. Judith Anderson played the title role. Asked why he was doing this show for a fraction of his

COUNTERPOINT (1967). With Maximilian Schell and Curt Lowens

usual salary, the actor answered: "It's a good part."

He refused a proposal to play Moshe Dayan on screen and, instead, signed up for what was to be his most successful movie since *Ben-Hur*.

Planet of the Apes, Pierre Boulle's allegorical novel about a futuristic world ruled by simians, had been purchased by Arthur P. Jacobs in 1963, but the producer was, for some time, unable to make a deal for any studio to finance the project. The industry consensus was that it would be impossible to have a cast full of talking monkeys on the screen without evoking hysterical laughter from the audience. Therefore the jokesters concluded that, if the book was to be filmed, it should be done by Walt Disney.

Richard Zanuck of Twentieth Century-Fox finally gave Jacobs the go-ahead for a test to see if a new make-up (created by John Chambers), which supposedly made actors appear as apes, while permitting them subtleties of expression, did indeed work. Volunteering their services for this

On television with Judith Anderson in
ELIZABETH THE QUEEN (1968)

experiment were Heston, playing a human astronaut, and Edward G. Robinson as a simian leader. The test was, of course, an enormous success, and the project was scheduled.

Heston was signed to play the spaceman, Taylor, in the 1968 film which was scripted by Michael Wilson and Rod Serling, and directed by Franklin J. Schaffner. The actor, in an interview with *Variety*'s Army Archerd, revealed that, in the past, he had turned down a number of science-fiction projects: "They were either pointers or followers—'Here they come or they went thataway'—but *Apes* is like *Gulliver's Travels*. It has a bitter satire within it. It shows how man can dehumanize man."

It was a truly innovative film, telling of three lost astronauts who land on a strange planet on which intelligent, talking apes dominate the caveman-level humans. Two of the travelers are quickly done away with by their hairy captors, but Heston, after undergoing an In-quisition, manages with the aid of some friendly chimps to escape to a territory forbidden to simians. It is there that he discovers he is, in fact, on Earth—hundreds of years after

PLANET OF THE APES (1968). Taylor is hosed down by the apes.

PLANET OF THE APES (1968). With Roddy McDowall and Kim Hunter

an atomic holocaust.

One of the most unforgettable scenes was Heston's trial. Stripped naked and unable to speak (his vocal cords had been temporarily impaired upon his capture), the frightened mortal listens helplessly as his judges decide that he is to be neutered. Later, he attempts to escape and, when recaptured, surprises the simians, who are unaware that humans can talk, by speaking his first words: "Get your hands off me, you dirty, stinking apes!"

As the cynical astronaut who eventually must reassert man's superiority over all other animals, Heston was splendid, but he was certainly overshadowed by the cast of exceptional players who donned monkey costumes. Roddy McDowall, Maurice Evans (replacing Edward G. Robinson, who found it too difficult to work in the cumbersome make-up), Kim Hunter, James Daly, and James Whitmore made their simian characters both frightening and believable. Indeed, within a very few minutes after the apes first appeared on the screen, audiences totally accepted these bizarre characters as real. A strong story, sure direction, and the scenic splendor of Utah and the Arizona National Park aided this critically acclaimed movie to achieve a domestic gross of $15 million.

The box-office prestige Heston may have garnered from the success of *Apes* was, more than likely, dissipated by the reception that welcomed his other 1968 picture, *Will Penny*. Even with raves from the nation's press, this Paramount Western was a financial disaster—yet it contains the star's finest screen performance to date.

Director Tom Gries' thoughtful and unusual tale concerned an aging cowpoke, who feels the stirrings of romance for the first time, yet walks away from the relationship, realizing it has no future. The film contained sufficient violence and suspense, motivated by a family of scavenging rawhiders, but the main thrust was the love story between the penniless Will Penny and the woman traveling across the plains with her young son to meet her partner in an unhappy marriage.

Action gave way to characterization in the Technicolor production, with Donald Pleasence portraying the lead villain with just the right amount of menace, and Joan Hackett giving a moving performance as the distraught lady. Heston, in the unglamorous role of an illiterate man with limited opportunities, turned in the most sterling performance. For a performer who usually played highly intelligent characters, this was a complete about-face, and Heston endowed Will Penny with a

WILL PENNY (1968). In the title role

WILL PENNY (1968). With Joan Hackett

vulnerability the public had never seen him display before.

Director Gries explains how he was able to draw such a sensitive performance out of Heston when others had failed: "Many directors are shy working with stars of large physical stature, but I discussed this part in detail with Chuck prior to filming, and told him I wanted him to play Penny *smaller* than life. The character must appear a frightened man.

"Chuck has some bad habits —some weaknesses as an actor. He is not a very relaxed man anyway,

so he grimaces a lot. He also has a tendency to play—emotionally—the end of a scene before he gets there.

"All during filming, I stood right behind the camera and, if he slipped into one of those habits, I'd call his attention to it."

Every opportunity to debunk the Western myths made popular by novelists and filmmakers over the years was seized by Gries to enhance this production. Early in the action, for example, Heston gets tired of a young trail hand refering to him as an "old man," and

NUMBER ONE (1969). As Ron ("Cat") Catlan

decides to take him on in a fight. But instead of employing Marquis of Queensbury rules and giving the punk a fair chance (in the style of Roy Rogers, Hopalong Cassidy, and, on occasion, even John Wayne), he stomps him with two blows—a swift kick in the rump, and a smack over the head with a heavy frying pan.

Moviegoers who got the opportunity to see *Will Penny* liked it, but since the bewildered studio heads had decided to write-off this out-of-the-ordinary Western and spend only a scant amount of money on promotion, attendance was virtually nil.

Heston's next picture, *Number One* (original titles: *Quarterback* and *Pro*) earned neither a good box-office return nor satisfactory notices. A 1969 release from United Artists, this character study of an over-the-hill football player who refuses to retire (inspired by the story of Y. A. Tittle of the New York Giants) was, like *The War Lord*, a project the actor had tried to get produced for several years. At one point, there was talk that comic Bill Cosby would co-star, but that possibility did not develop. Heston finally did get the story before the cameras by agreeing to accept a small salary ($4000) plus a percentage of the profits—of which there were ultimately none.

Handsomely mounted and featuring the participation of the New Orleans Saints, *Number One*, nevertheless, was burdened by David Moessinger's dull, cliché-ridden script which director ·Tom Gries was unable to inject with much life. Heston, appearing much more stoic than he had in his last few films, did create a certain sympathy for the aging athlete, Ron "Cat" Catlan, but the more interesting performances came from Jessica Walter, as his fashion-designer wife, and Diana Muldaur, playing a woman with whom he has a short-lived affair.

A particularly hard-hitting scene had Heston, in the stadium parking lot, being approached by a former teammate, who is down on his luck. Heston gives this once top player all the cash in his pocket, and viewers can read on his face the fear of being in a similar position in the not-too-distant future. In this light, the final shot of the picture is sobering, showing a badly injured Heston—blood streaming from his ear—lying unconscious on the playing field.

Speaking in his capacity as SAG President, Heston addressed a government commission in May of 1970, which was studying pornography and ways to combat it. He said, in part: "The problem would seem to be, initially, at least, one of definition. Nearly everyone seems willing to agree that pornography should be controlled, but almost no one can agree on what pornography is . . .

"I don't think that filmmakers as a group can be held responsible for the production of pornography movies any more than the public as a whole can be held responsible for their success. The public will get, by and large, those films it has shown it will pay to see.

"Even *Oedipus* and *Lysistrata* are not appropriate fare for seven-year-old girls. I think the film industry has responded very well to their responsibility with the rating code. . . . The healthiest art is the freest, and most diverse art. This is what the artist wants, and what the public deserves."

As a favor to producer Arthur Jacobs, Heston agreed to briefly reprise the role of Taylor in the slap-dash 1970 release, *Beneath the Planet of the Apes* (original titles: *Planet of the Apes Revisited* and *Planet of the Men*), the first of four sequels to the original 1968 hit. James Franciscus was the actual star, playing an astronaut searching for Heston, who appeared at the film's end to confront Maurice Evans once again, then blow up the evil planet. Heston's undemanding role took only a week to shoot.

Inexpensively produced, from a script by Paul Dehn, *Beneath* was directed by Ted Post and, in addition to Evans, featured Kim Hunter and Linda Harrison (as Heston's cave-girl romantic interest) in a replay of their original parts. Dialogue, acting, and direction may have been substandard, but the movie still earned a substantial sum at the box office.

The star's next movie was also a sequel, although he had not appeared in the original film. *The Hawaiians* (1970) continued James Michener's epic novel, which had been dramatized, in part, in the 1966 production, *Hawaii*. Heston played Whip Hoxworth, grandson of the character essayed by Richard Harris in 1966.

Directed at a leisurely pace by Tom Gries from James R. Webb's often interesting, albeit superficial and confusing screenplay, the beautifully photographed film told how the Chinese came to settle and gain influence on the Pacific island group. Unfortunately, Heston, playing the wealthy landowner who introduces the pineapple to Hawaii as a commercial crop, seemed to simply walk through his assignment, looking strong and handsome, but giving no suggestion of depth in the character. (Tom Gries: "I was annoyed with Chuck on this picture. He was preparing to direct *Antony and Cleopatra* at the time and, frankly, his mind was more on that than on *The Hawaiians*.") Much better was Tina Chen, brilliant as the young Chinese immi-

BENEATH THE PLANET OF THE APES (1970). With Linda Harrison

THE HAWAIIANS (1970). As Whip Hoxworth

grant girl who ages in the movie into a powerful matriarch.

Undiscriminating audiences may have enjoyed this episodic United Artists release, which was enhanced by a realistic re-creation of Hawaii of the 1800s (including a $300,000 reproduction of Honolulu's Chinatown), but nonetheless, it failed at the box office.

In an interview with Bob Thomas of *Associated Press*, Heston stated: "It's important for an actor not to be associated with big losers. . . . If you are the star of a picture that lays a big bomb, that's when your collar gets tight. The bankers start saying, 'Oh, yes, he's the guy in the picture that lost all that money.' " Regrettably, at this point in his career, some of the movie moguls were saying this about Heston.

Before doing *The Hawaiians*, Heston had traveled to England, then Spain, and there had recreated the role of Marc Antony in a new film rendition of Shakespeare's *Julius Caesar*. Released by American International in August of 1970—two months after the Michener picture had hit the theaters—this production was, for the most part, filled with strong performances by an internationally known cast.

Heston, more subdued and laconic than he had been in Bradley's *Julius Caesar*, was quite impressive as the avenging Antony,

giving many of the familiar lines unusual, yet valid, readings. Richard Johnson as Cassius (replacing previously announced Richard Harris), John Gielgud as Caesar, Diana Rigg as Portia, and Jill Bennett as Calpurnia were also superb in their roles.

Only Jason Robards, a fine stage actor who has, sadly, never been able to effectively adapt his unusual talent to celluloid, was a detriment to the roster of players. Playing the pivotal part of Brutus, Robards—with his New York accent—read virtually all of his lines in a monotone, destroying the dramatic effect of every scene he was in. It was a totally deadpan portrayal, devoid of feeling or sensitivity.

Not that the movie itself was anything to get excited about. Production values included tacky costumes and cramped sets, as well as clumsily staged battle scenes reminiscent of those found in "spaghetti" Westerns. Stuart Burge's direction was more academic than innovative and the picture moved at a sluggish pace.

Heston's next film was a remake of *The Last Man on Earth*, a 1964 Vincent Price science-fiction movie from AIP, which had, in turn, been based on a chilling novel by Richard Matheson entitled *I Am Legend*. Warner Brothers acquired the rights to the original material

THE HAWAIIANS (1970). With Geraldine Chaplin

JULIUS CAESAR (1970). Antony and his soldiers

THE OMEGA MAN (1971). As Neville, surrounded by enemy beings

and, in July of 1971, released *The Omega Man*, in which Heston played a man who, at first, appears to be the only normal survivor in a world that had been decimated by germ warfare.

Wandering about a deserted Los Angeles, Heston battles "the Family," a group of bizarre nocturnal mutants, who are pledged to avenge their fate by destroying all remnants of technology. Since Heston is a scientist, who escaped the deadly plague by injecting himself with an experimental vaccine, he is the society's target.

The production had several attributes: snatches of sharp, amusing dialogue; a talented supporting cast, especially Anthony Zerbe as the mutant leader; efficient direction by Boris Sagal; and some truly impressive scenes, such as Charlton's moving through the metropolis—empty except for decaying corpses.

On the negative side was an intermittently moving, otherwise pallid, performance by Heston; a screenplay that held viewer interest, but also slipped back-and-forth between being a slam-bang action thriller and a heavy message film; and a score by Ron Grainer that would have been more appropriate in a television travelogue.

More than once, the picture's attempt at symbolism backfired, drawing unwanted laughter from audiences. Heston's death scene,

ANTONY AND CLEOPATRA (1972). With Hildegarde Neil

for instance, with the star run through by a spear, lying with arms outstretched and legs crossed, was too much like Jesus on the Cross to be taken seriously.

When, in 1971, he retired as President of the Screen Actors' Guild, Heston was presented with that union's annual award "for outstanding achievement in fostering the finest ideals of the acting profession."

Heston had, for years, scoffed at the idea of directing a film, but he finally agreed to take the plunge on a production of Shakespeare's *Antony and Cleopatra* (1972), which had, of course, been his first Broadway production back in 1947.

Approached by producer Peter Snell to just play Antony, Heston told the *Los Angeles Times* that he had become a first-time director by default: "When Peter and I first started plans for the project, we cast around trying to think of someone to direct. Most film directors do not know Shakespeare and most Shakespearean directors do not know film—with the obvious exceptions of Olivier and Orson Welles, neither of whom was available. I have done as much Shakespeare as any American director, and I have also made thirty-seven films and I would hope that some of it has rubbed off.

"The basis of the advice I received from both Welles and Olivier prior to beginning production was that we should get very professional, very disciplined actors for all the major roles and that I also must have a good actor to double for me. You have to be able to watch the scene when you are not acting, but it has to be well acted."

He worked for months in designing this project—first doing his own adaptation of Shakespeare's words, then blocking out the picture's movement. Much of this preparation, in fact, took place while he was playing in other films.

Shot in Spain in beautiful Technicolor and Todd A035, the production received a release through Rank. Unknown Hildegarde Neil was Cleopatra (instead of first choices Anne Bancroft or Irene Papas) in a cast that included Eric Porter, John Castle, and Fernando Rey. To date, with the exception of a single showing in Washington, D.C., the production has not played the United States.

It did show elsewhere, however, but reviews were less than flattering. The *London Evening Standard* wrote: ". . . Unfortunately, decent intentions don't redeem a dull film devoid of imagination, shorn of poetry and utterly lacking in the sexual chemistry that must work between the title figures if it's to be more than a long haul to the tomb."

"I have no further plans to

SKYJACKED (1972). As Capt. Henry O'Hara

SKYJACKED (1972). Capt. O'Hara under the gun

direct," said Heston after completing this picture. "If another opportunity like this one occurred where I knew there was a need for me to be the director and there was a part in that project which I could conveniently do as an actor, then perhaps I would consider it. But I am still primarily and happily an actor."

Having done *Antony and Cleopatra* for merely a participation in any profits, Heston realized that he had to do a couple of films for *money*, so he signed to star in MGM's taut thriller, *Skyjacked* (working title: *Airborne*), which was rushed into release early in 1972 to take advantage of the then topical trend toward aerial piracy.

Produced in Metrocolor by Walter Seltzer, who had previously been associated with Heston on pictures like *Will Penny, Number One* and *The Omega Man*, the movie told how a psychotic military man (effectively portrayed by James Brolin) commandeers a jetliner—occupied by an all-star cast—and forces the captain (Heston) to fly him to Russia, with a refueling stop along the way in Alaska. John Guillermin, directing Stanley R. Greenberg's suspenseful screenplay (from a novel by David Harper) on a relatively low but sufficient budget, created an exciting, well-acted entertainment—one of the best edge-of-the-seat films.

For Heston, this was a familiar role: the strong, brave leader who must resolve a very tense situation. It was an easy assignment for him to handle, and if Guillermin ever gave them a chance to catch their breath, audiences knew that, with Heston at the controls, there was nothing much to worry about.

Heston next journeyed to Oslo, Norway, to assume the leading role in an Italian/French/German/Spanish remake of Jack London's *Call of the Wild*. Though shot in 1972, the picture was not released in the United States until 1976. The screenplay by Hubert Frank and Tibor Reves, directed by Ken Annakin, related how two Alaskan roughnecks (Heston and Italo-Western hero George Eastman) are continually helped out of difficulty by Buck, a sheepdog by nature, but in his ability to save lives, a St. Bernard. Dog fights, sled chases, saloon brawls, and similar sequences provided audiences with plenty of action.

Variety gave the picture a very bad review, citing major script problems and inadequate performances by supporting players. The notice concluded with: "It's not what one has come to expect of an Annakin film and one featuring Charlton Heston."

Heston's reaction to the finished production: "The *dog* was good."

SOYLENT GREEN (1973). With Edward G. Robinson

SOYLENT GREEN (1973). With Chuck Connors

On December 5th, Heston was back on stage, opening at Los Angeles' Ahmanson Theatre in a production of *The Crucible*, Arthur Miller's drama of the Salem witch trials. Joseph Hardy directed a cast that included Inga Swenson, James Olson, Beah Richards, and Gale Sondergaard. Writing in the *Los Angeles Times*, Dan Sullivan noted that Heston gave a "strong but flexible performance" as John Proctor, the play's central character.

Since most of his financially successful films of the last decade had been in the genre of science-fiction, Heston found no reason to turn down another of these—*Soylent Green* (1973), a disturbing look at life (circa 2022) in the over-populated, smog-insulated police state called New York. Here, in this rioting city, real food is a luxury item and even the supply of synthetic food from the sea is becoming scarce. A new source of sustenance—Soylent Green—appears on the market. But what is this strange new product made from?

Heston played a New York

police detective, investigating the assassination murder of industrialist Joseph Cotten, who had discovered the shocking secret of the Soylent Corporation. Ignoring warnings from his superiors to stay away from the mystery, the cop continues to pursue the solution, and encounters even more violent attempts to dissuade him.

Like *The Omega Man*, the MGM release had a script by Stanley R. Greenberg (from Harry Harrison's novel), which could not decide whether it should be an abstract intellectual movie or a straight actioner. Richard Fleischer's overly restrained direction did not help to alleviate the problem.

The film's strongest assets were the interesting, well-executed performances. Heston, though grimacing occasionally, was convincing as the prototype for the doomed average man of the future; Leigh Taylor-Young scored as the femme interest, a "piece of furniture" who serves as the mistress to whoever rents her quarters in a luxury apartment building; and Chuck Connors was menacing as Cotten's disloyal bodyguard.

Walking away with the acting honors, however, was Edward G. Robinson in his final screen role as an elderly police researcher or "book." His last scene, in which he undergoes a peaceful death in the futuristic suicide pleasure dome amid a Cinerama-type presentation of a world of trees, fresh water, and wildlife that no longer exist, was the picture's highlight.

Despite its downbeat, awkwardly developed story, *Soylent Green* was a rather intriguing, often entertaining production, which many moviegoers enjoyed. Regrettably, box-office returns broke no records.

Charlton Heston was a survivor, maintaining his career and star status these last few years through a seldom-broken string of financial flops. But now his filmic fortunes were about to take an upward turn.

"**G**reat men are more interesting to play than ordinary men," Heston told interviewers while he was filming *The Three Musketeers* (1974) in Spain. The actor was playing the role of Cardinal Richelieu, "the architect of modern France," and finding it to be one of his most challenging undertakings.

"The main problem," he continued, "was one of physical bulk. Richelieu was not a muscular man, and he was plagued with health problems all his life which he surmounted with iron will. Besides skin ulcers, he suffered from migraines, so much so, in fact, that in the famous Philippe de Champagne portrait, you can see his temple vein quite clearly.

"The part did daunt me a bit, but an actor must use his own equipment. Some actors are gifted with neutral equipment, like Alec Guinness who can readily suggest a shy clerk to a major general. I didn't have that luxury here."

To overcome his own robustness, Heston developed a limp, although there is no historical record that the controversial cleric had one ("It's sort of an acronym of his ills") and also spoke with a slighter voice than his own. In addition, he wore a false nose that narrowed and elongated his face: "It's the first time in my career that I've ever used one, but Richelieu is the first historical figure I've ever played

who had a bigger nose than I have."

Richelieu must be counted as one of Heston's most interesting screen assignments. As the nefarious, though shrewd Cardinal, he managed to subdue many of his well-known mannerisms and create a character unlike any he had ever played before. It was a satisfying and believable portrayal.

The film itself had sprung from the clever minds of producer Ilya Salkind and director Richard Lester, who, at one point, had toyed with the idea of casting the Beatles in this zany, satirical remake of the Dumas classic. Later, when it became apparent that the rock group was not available, an international all-star cast was assembled to play the key roles—Michael York as D'Artagnan; Oliver Reed, Richard Chamberlain, and Frank Finlay in the title roles; and Raquel Welch, Faye Dunaway, and Geraldine Chaplin appearing in the principal feminine parts.

The screenplay by George MacDonald Fraser took a rather clever tongue-in-cheek approach to the familiar adventure yarn. Indeed, the Lester/Fraser view of the renowned musketeers was that they were more interested in money, women, and friendship than undue fidelity to their simple-minded king, amusingly played by

THE THREE MUSKETEERS (1974). With Faye Dunaway

Jean-Pierre Cassell. The heroic D'Artagnan, on the other hand, was little more than a country bumpkin.

A Fox release in color, *The Three Musketeers* earned positive reviews from the nation's press. Only the purists objected to this project, claiming that it was not a *true* swashbuckler because it appeared that none of the principals really knew the proper use of swords . . . or, if they did, Lester instructed them not to make that knowledge obvious.

The filmmakers' original intent was to tell Dumas' saga in one movie, but once the exposed film arrived in the editing room, it was discovered that the picture would run over 3½ hours. Ergo, Salkind and Lester divided the footage, releasing the second half of the movie a year after the first. *The Three Musketeers* was subtitled *The Queen's Diamonds*, while *The Four Musketeers* (1975), featuring the same cast enacting the remaining portion of the book, was tagged *The Revenge of Milady*. To placate actors protesting that they had signed for only *one* movie, the producers negotiated a participation in profits arrangement with the stars on the second release. Like most sequels, *The Four Musketeers* was not as successful as its predecessor, though it was certainly a box-office hit.

After he had completed filming

THE FOUR MUSKETEERS (1975). As Cardinal Richelieu

THE FOUR MUSKETEERS (1975). With Jean Pierre Cassell

for Salkind in Spain, Heston accepted offers to star in a pair of disaster pictures back-to-back at Universal. Neither role was particularly demanding of his talents, and, in both productions, though top-billed, he was merely one of a long list of major stars. However, the two efforts were—except for *The Ten Commandments* and *Ben-Hur*—the most financially successful (to date) in his career.

The first to be shot, though released a month after the other, was *Earthquake* (1974). Produced and directed by Mark Robson in a deafening new process known as

"Sensurround," the story followed the intertwined lives of a varied group of people on the day that a killer earthquake levels Los Angeles. All the performances were well drawn, with Heston playing a successful architect, married to the boss' disturbed daughter (Ava Gardner) and having an affair with Genevieve Bujold. Lorne Greene was his father-in-law, and the cast also featured George Kennedy as a cop, Richard Roundtree playing a motorcycle daredevil and Marjoe Gortner as a psychotic. Even Walter Matthau—billed as Matuschanskayasky—made a gag ppearance in the part of a drunk.

George Fox and Mario Puzo fashioned an engrossing screenplay or this $7-million epic, brimming with stock but colorful characters. They then turned it over to Mark Robson, who, with the aid of the studio's multitalented special effects department, created one of the most exciting and frightening (especially for Los Angeles residents) films to hit the theaters in some time.

This picture, with its burning, thundering, crashing, spitting, roaring horror of a catastrophic earthquake, gave the public food for thought. A speech of architect Heston's as he surveyed the destruction about him ("For the first time in my life, I'm ashamed for my profession. Why do we build these forty-story monstrosities?") regularly drew applause from audiences.

His most effective scene in the picture came at the climax when, while climbing out of the rapidly flooding sewer (a nearby dam had given way as a result of the quake), he must decide whether to save himself or dive back into the rushing water to rescue wife Gardner. Gazing almost apologetically at Miss Bujold for one last time, he jumps in after Gardner and the pair quickly disappear from sight.

Obviously, since this movie could have easily concluded on a happier note without damaging the inte-

EARTHQUAKE (1974). With Lorne Greene and Ava Gardner

EARTHQUAKE (1974). With George Kennedy

EARTHQUAKE (1974). With Monica Lewis

grity of the story, one wonders if the choice to kill off Heston was made simply to dispute his critics who were commenting that, on the screen, he was virtually invincible.

Airport 1975 (1974) was a successful attempt by Universal to capitalize on their previous huge moneymaker, *Airport*. It was directed by Jack Smight from an original script by Don Ingalls. Aside from the title, however, the only carryover from the original film and Arthur Hailey's best-selling book was the character of Operations Head Joe Petroni, played in both movies by George Kennedy.

The basic premise of this picture was a mid-air collision in which the flight crew of a 747 jet airliner i either killed or badly injured necessitating that a new pilot b lowered from a jet helicopter to th damaged aircraft. A host of cele brity names—Karen Black, Gloria Swanson, Efrem Zimbalist, Jr. Susan Clark, Helen Reddy, Myrna Loy, Sid Caesar, and Dana Andrews—played the people involve in the disaster; none of them however, due to the limitations o the superficial screenplay, was abl to develop a character of any depth and merely treated audiences to a replay of his or her well-established persona.

Heston's role, of course, was tha

AIRPORT 1975 (1974). With Ed Nelson

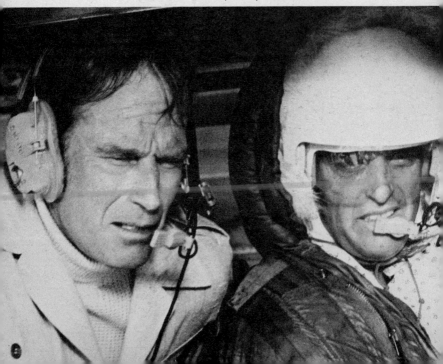

AIRPORT 1975 (1974). With Karen Black

of the replacement pilot, lowered from the helicopter after another man had been killed in a similar attempt. Looking very intense and grimacing a lot, Heston, as expected, saved the day. However, he couldn't save a trite script with often unintentionally laughable dialogue. (Interesting sidelight: In *The Crowded Sky*, made in 1960, Efrem Zimbalist, Jr. played the pilot of a small military jet that crashed into an airliner flown by Dana Andrews. *Airport 1975* had the actors reversing roles. Andrews was flying the smaller craft that collided with pilot Zimbalist's jetliner.)

Heston was one of the first performers approached to star in Universal's blockbuster, *Jaws*; however, the deal never got out of negotiations: "The studio, quite correctly, decided they didn't need to give an actor a percentage of the gross."

There was talk of his appearing in Ibsen's *An Enemy of the People* for Ely Landau's innovative American Film Theatre, but, unfortunately, that organization folded after its second season. Instead, he signed to star with Vanessa Red-

MIDWAY (1976). With Henry Fonda

grave in a new staging of Shakespeare's *Macbeth*, which opened at the Ahmanson Theatre in Los Angeles in January of 1975. Directed by Peter Wood, with a supporting cast that featured Richard Jordan as Macduff and John Ireland as Duncan, the production was "roasted" by many of the local critics. Dan Sullivan of the *Los Angeles Times* said that Heston's performance was "as featureless as an annual report and as slow-pouring as motor oil at 15 below zero."

With his last four releases—*The Three Musketeers, Airport 1975, Earthquake*, and *The Four Musketeers*—all major box-office hits, Heston's "bankability" with film investors has increased and more lucrative offers have rolled in. At the time of this writing, in fact, the actor has five pictures in various stages of pre-release:

Midway, a Universal production, is scheduled to open during the summer of 1976. Set against the background of the epic naval battle that turned the tide for the

THE LAST HARD MEN (1976). With Christopher Mitchum

With wife Lydia in 1972

United States in the Pacific in World War II, the film has a screenplay by Donàld S. Sanford, direction by Jack Smight and, like such movies as *The Longest Day* and *Tora! Tora! Tora!*, a stellar cast: Henry Fonda, James Coburn, Glenn Ford, Hal Holbrook, Toshiro Mifune, Robert Mitchum, Cliff Robertson, and Robert Wagner.

Discussing his part in *Midway*, Heston commented: "Oddly enough, in this picture I'm not playing an historical role, but almost everyone else is. I've come to feel that the character is not really fictional but rather anonymous. I'm playing a navy officer who stands well enough for the hundreds and hundreds of unknown officers and men who fought and performed admirably at Midway."

The Last Hard Men, also scheduled for 1976 release, is a Western from Twentieth Century-Fox. Set in Arizona of 1909, it stars Heston as a retired lawman who goes back into action to rescue his kidnapped daughter (Barbara Hershey) from longtime nemesis James Coburn. Christopher Mitchum, Jorge Rivero, and Michael Parks play important roles in the Guerdon Trueblood screenplay, based on a novel by Brian Garfield. Andrew V. McLaglen is the director.

Mitchum, the youngest son of ac-

tor Robert Mitchum, describes Heston as "a sincere, genuine man who gives you all he can when playing a scene." The two actors played a constant chess game during the off-camera time on this production—with Chris constantly defeating the star, who, after a weekend trip home, brought back his own chess set, because he was "more used to it." This change, nor Mitchum's spotting Heston a piece in each game, didn't make much difference. He still lost, and finally announced that he could beat Chris if he could play on a larger board.

The young actor bought Heston a new set—thirty inches on a side, with five-inch high pieces—and gave it to him with a note: "If this is too small, you take the Americas. . . ."

This did the trick. Heston won the next game and, at the end of production, presented Chris with a photo of himself, bent over a chess board. The caption read: ". . . Now if I just move Mitchum's rook over two squares before he gets back . . ."

Tentatively set for 1976 release is another Universal picture, *Two-Minute Warning*, which has Heston in the role of a Los Angeles police captain, out to stop a sniper who is hiding above a jam-packed football stadium and shooting spectators at random. A novel by George La Fountaine served as the basis for

Edward Hume's script, directed by Larry Peerce. Concentrating on the innocent victims of this senseless violence, rather than the sniper himself, the production co-stars John Cassavetes, Martin Balsam, Beau Bridges, Marilyn Hassett, David Janssen, Jack Klugman, and Gena Rowlands.

Another tentative 1976 release is a new version of Mark Twain's *The Prince and the Pauper*, a perennial favorite for the movies, with previous versions in 1909, 1915, 1923, 1937, and 1962. Heston is scheduled to play King Henry VIII in this all-star production with George C. Scott, Raquel Welch, Rex Harrison, Ernest Borgnine, Mark Lester, and Oliver Reed in other central roles.

In February of 1976, Hollywood trade papers announced that, beginning in July, Heston would start shooting his fifty-second motion picture, *Gray Lady Down*, with an original screenplay by James Whittaker, that deals with the sinking of a nuclear submarine. The star's role is that of the ship's captain.

"I sometimes feel like one of the last surviving saber-toothed tigers," Heston told *Coronet* near the end of 1975, "lifting his nose and smelling the chill of the glaciers coming down from northern Europe. One day you start to look around and say, 'Hey, where did everyone from my crowd go?'

"I guess relishing what you do must be part of longevity because if your work starts to bore you, it shows. But I can't argue with actors who say acting is no longer a challenge to them. I think we're all uneasily aware that it's really kid's work. Acting is pretending, and pretending is what children do. And I'd be the last to make a case for it as a proper activity for grownups. But I *like* it. And I've been extremely fortunate doing it because I've been able to support my family and send my children to school . . . and get people to take down all my opinions and print them."

Neither critical barbs nor box-office bombs have seemed to measurably impede the career progress of Charlton Heston since he first came to Hollywood over a quarter century ago. His longevity has baffled detractors, while others with a more humorous bent joke that, ever since he played Moses, a "very influential supporter" has been in his corner.

Somebody once said, "Don't argue with success," and perhaps this is the rule that should apply here. Whether it is through the good fortune of having been cast in some very important pictures or the fact that he is a solidly professional actor whose colleagues enjoy working with him, Heston has made it big in the film industry and one must respect him for that accomplishment.

Yet of even greater significance, as one of the most believable portrayers of strong, virile, and heroic roles on the screen today, he has provided us with countless hours of solid entertainment, which is really what the movies are all about.

BIBLIOGRAPHY

Dew, Joan. "Charlton Heston Reveals," *Coronet*, November, 1975.

Gow, Gordon, "Actor's Country," *Films and Filming,* May, 1972.

Hamill, P. "Heston; Larger than Life," *Saturday Evening Post,* July 3, 1965.

Higham, Charles. *Ava.* Delacorte Press, New York, 1974.

Madsen, Axel. *William Wyler.* Thomas Y. Crowell Co., New York, 1973.

Martin, Pete. "I Call on Ben-Hur," *Saturday Evening Post,* August 20, 1960.

McClelland, Doug. *The Unkindest Cuts.* A.S. Barnes, Cranbury, New Jersey, 1972.

Shay, Don. *Conversations.* Kleidoscope Press, Albuquerque, 1969.

Shipman, David. *The Great Movie Stars: The International Years.* Crown Publishers, New York, 1970.

THE FILMS OF CHARLTON HESTON

The director's name follows the release date. A (c) following the release date indicates that the film is in color. Sp indicates Screenplay and b/o indicates based/on.

1. PEER GYNT. Brandon, 1941. *David Bradley.* Sp: Bradley, b/o play by Henrik Ibsen. Cast: Betty Hanisee, Mrs. Herbert Hyde, Lucielle Powell, Sue Straub, Charles Paetow, Kathryne Elfstrom, Morris Wilson, Betty Barton, Francis X. Bushman, Rose Andrews, and Alan Eckhart.

2. JULIUS CAESAR. Avon, 1949. *David Bradley.* Sp: Bradley, b/o play by William Shakespeare. Cast: Harold Tasker, Robert Holt, David Bradley, Grosvenor Glenn, William Russell, Helen Ross, Mary Darr, George Hinners, Arthur Sus, Cornelius Peeples, and Don Walker.

3. DARK CITY. Paramount, 1950. *William Dieterle.* Sp: John Meredyth Lucas and Larry Marcus, adaptation by Ketti Frings from story by Marcus. Cast: Lizabeth Scott, Viveca Lindfors, Dean Jagger, Don DeFore, Jack Webb, Ed Begley, Henry Morgan, Walter Sande, Mark Keuning, and Mike Mazurki.

4. THE GREATEST SHOW ON EARTH. Paramount, 1952 (c). *Cecil B. DeMille.* Sp: Fredric M. Frank, Barre Lyndon, and Theodore St. John, b/o story by Frank Cavett, Frank, and St. John. Cast: Betty Hutton, Cornel Wilde, Dorothy Lamour, Gloria Grahame, James Stewart, Henry Wilcoxon, Lyle Bettger, Lawrence Tierney, Emmett Kelly, John Ringling North, and John Kellogg.

5. THE SAVAGE. Paramount, 1952 (c). *George Marshall.* Sp: Sydney Boehm, b/o novel by L.L. Foreman. Cast: Susan Morrow, Peter Hanson, Richard Rober, Joan Taylor, Donald Porter, Ted De Corsia, Ian MacDonald, and Milburn Stone.

6. RUBY GENTRY. 20th Century-Fox, 1952. *King Vidor.* Sp: Sylvia Richards, b/o story by Arthur Fitz-Richard. Cast: Jennifer Jones, Karl Malden, Tom Tully, Bernard Phillips, James Anderson, Josephine Hutchinson, Phyllis Avery, Herbert Heyes, Myra Marsh, and Sam Flint.

7.   PONY EXPRESS. Paramount, 1953 (c). *Jerry Hopper.* Sp: Charles Marquis Warren, b/o story by Frank Gruber. Cast: Rhonda Fleming, Jan Sterling, Forrest Tucker, Michael Moore, Porter Hall, Richard Shannon, Henry Brandon, and Stuart Randall.

8.   THE PRESIDENT'S LADY. 20th Century-Fox, 1953. *Henry Levin.* Sp: John Patrick, b/o novel by Irving Stone. Cast: Susan Hayward, John McIntire, Fay Bainter, Whitfield Connor, Ruth Attaway, Ralph Dumke, Margaret Wycherly, Carl Betz, and Nina Varela.

9.   ARROWHEAD. Paramount, 1953 (c). *Charles Marquis Warren.* Sp: Warren, b/o novel by W. R. Burnett. Cast: Jack Palance, Katy Jurado, Brian Keith, Mary Sinclair, Milburn Stone, Richard Shannon, Lewis Martin, and Frank de Kova.

10.   BAD FOR EACH OTHER. Columbia, 1953. *Irving Rapper.* Sp: Irving Wallace and Horace McCoy, b/o novel by McCoy. Cast: Lizabeth Scott, Dianne Foster, Mildred Dunnock, Arthur Franz, Ray Collins, Marjorie Rambeau, Lester Matthews, and Rhys Williams.

11.   THE NAKED JUNGLE. Paramount, 1954 (c). *Byron Haskin.* Sp: Philip Yordan and Ranald MacDougall, b/o story by Carl Stephenson. Cast: Eleanor Parker, Abraham Sofaer, William Conrad, Romo Vincent, Douglas Fowley, John Dierkes, and Leonard Strong.

12.   SECRET OF THE INCAS. Paramount, 1954 (c). *Jerry Hopper.* Sp: Ranald MacDougall and Sydney Boehm, b/o story by Boehm. Cast: Robert Young, Nicole Maurey, Thomas Mitchell, Yma Sumac, Glenda Farrell, Michael Pate, Leon Askin, William Henry, Kurt Katch, and Marion Ross.

13.   THE FAR HORIZONS. Paramount, 1955 (c). *Rudolph Maté.* Sp: Winston Miller and Edmund H. North, b/o novel by Della Gould Emmons. Cast: Fred MacMurray, Donna Reed, Barbara Hale, William Demarest, Alan Reed, Eduardo Noriega, Larry Pennell, Ralph Moody, Herbert Heyes, and Lester Matthews.

14.   THE PRIVATE WAR OF MAJOR BENSON. Universal, 1955 (c). *Jerry Hopper.* Sp: William Roberts and Richard Alan Simmons, b/o story by Joe Connelly and Bob Mosher. Cast: Julie Adams, William Demarest, Tim Considine, Sal Mineo, Nana Bryant, Kay Stewart, Mary Field, Tim Hovey, Milburn Stone, and Don Haggerty.

15.   LUCY GALLANT. Paramount, 1955 (c). *Robert Parrish*. Sp: John Lee Mahin and Winston Miller, b/o novel by Margaret Cousins. Cast: Jane Wyman, Claire Trevor, Thelma Ritter, William Demarest, Wallace Ford, Tom Helmore, Gloria Talbott, James Westerfield, and Mary Field.

16.   THE TEN COMMANDMENTS. Paramount, 1956 (c). *Cecil B. DeMille*. Sp: Aeneas MacKenzie, Jesse L. Lasky, Jr.., Jack Gariss, and Fredric M. Frank. Cast: Yul Brynner, Anne Baxter, Edward G. Robinson, Yvonne De Carlo, Debra Paget, John Derek, Sir Cedric Hardwicke, Nina Foch, Martha Scott, Judith Anderson, Vincent Price, John Carradine, Olive Deering, Henry Wilcoxon, Eduard Franz, H.B. Warner, Woodrow Strode, and Fraser Heston. Previously filmed in 1923.

17.   THREE VIOLENT PEOPLE. Paramount, 1957 (c). *Rudolph Maté*. Sp: James Edward Grant, b/o story by Leonard Praskins and Barney Slater. Cast: Anne Baxter, Gilbert Roland, Tom Tryon, Forrest Tucker, Bruce Bennett, Elaine Stritch, and Barton MacLane.

18.   TOUCH OF EVIL. Universal, 1958. *Orson Welles*. Sp: Welles, b/o novel by Whit Masterson. Cast: Janet Leigh, Orson Welles, Joseph Calleia, Akim Tamiroff, Joanna Moore, Ray Collins, Dennis Weaver, Valentin De Vargas, Mort Mills, Joseph Cotten, Zsa Zsa Gabor, Marlene Dietrich, and Keenan Wynn.

19.   THE BIG COUNTRY. United Artists, 1958 (c). *William Wyler*. Sp: James R. Webb. Sy Bartlett, and Robert Wilder, b/o novel by Donald Hamilton. Cast: Gregory Peck, Jean Simmons, Carroll Baker, Burl Ives, Charles Bickford, Alfonso Bedoya, Chuck Connors, Chuck Hayward, Buff Brady, Jim Burk, and Dorothy Adams.

20.   THE BUCCANEER. Paramount, 1958 (c). *Anthony Quinn*. Sp: Jesse L. Lasky, Jr. and Bernice Mosk, b/o screenplay by Harold Lamb, Edwin Justus Mayer, and C. Gardner Sullivan, and book by Lyle Saxon. Cast: Yul Brynner, Claire Bloom, Charles Boyer, Inger Stevens, Henry Hull, E.G. Marshall, Lorne Greene, Ted DeCorsia, Douglass Dumbrille, and Fran Jeffries. Previous filmed in 1938.

21.   BEN-HUR. MGM, 1959 (c). *William Wyler*. Sp: Karl Tunberg, b/o novel by Lew Wallace. Cast: Jack Hawkins, Haya Harareet, Stephen Boyd, Hugh Griffith, Martha Scott, Cathy O'Donnell, Sam Jaffe, Finlay Currie, Frank Thring, Terence Longdon, George Relph, Andre Morell, Marina Berti, Adi Berber, and Jose Greci. Previously filmed in 1927.

22. THE WRECK OF THE MARY DEARE. MGM, 1959 (c). *Michael Anderson*. Sp: Eric Ambler, b/o novel by Hammond Innes. Cast: Gary Cooper, Michael Redgrave, Emlyn Williams, Cecil Parker, Alexander Knox, Virginia McKenna, Richard Harris, Ben Wright, and Charles Davis.

23. EL CID. Allied Artists, 1961 (c). *Anthony Mann*. Sp: Fredric M. Frank and Philip Yordan. Cast: Sophia Loren, Raf Vallone, Genevieve Page, John Fraser, Gary Raymond, Hurd Hatfield, Massimo Serato, Herbert Lom, Frank Thring, Douglas Wilmer, Michael Hordern, and Ralph Truman.

24. THE PIGEON THAT TOOK ROME. Paramount, 1962. *Melville Shavelson*. Sp: Shavelson, b/o novel by Donald Downes. Cast: Elsa Martinelli, Harry Guardino, Baccaloni, Marietto, Gabriella Pallotta, Debbie Price, Brian Donlevy, and Arthur Shields.

25. DIAMOND HEAD. Columbia, 1962 (c). *Guy Green*. Sp: Marguerite Roberts, b/o novel by Peter Gilman. Cast: Yvette Mimieux, George Chakiris, France Nuyen, James Darren, Aline MacMahon, Elizabeth Allen, Vaughn Taylor, Marc Marno, Philip Ahn, and Harold Fong.

26. 55 DAYS AT PEKING. Allied Artists, 1963 (c). *Nicholas Ray*. Sp: Philip Yordan and Bernard Gordon. Cast: Ava Gardner, David Niven, Flora Robson, John Ireland, Harry Andrews, Leo Genn, Robert Helpmann, Kurt Kasznar, Paul Lukas, Lynne Sue Moon, Jerome Thor, Elizabeth Sellars, and Jacques Sernas.

27. THE GREATEST STORY EVER TOLD. United Artists, 1965 (c). *George Stevens*. Sp: James Lee Barrett, Stevens, and Carl Sandburg, b/o the Holy Bible, the book by Fulton Oursler, and writings by Henry Denker. Cast: Max Von Sydow, Dorothy McGuire, Robert Blake, David Hedison, David McCallum, Roddy McDowall, Ina Balin, Sidney Poitier, Carroll Baker, Pat Boone, Van Heflin, Sal Mineo, Shelley Winters, Michael Ansara, Ed Wynn, John Wayne, Telly Savalas, Angela Lansbury, Joseph Schildkraut, Victor Buono, José Ferrer, Claude Rains, Donald Pleasence, and Richard Conte.

28. MAJOR DUNDEE. Columbia, 1965 (c). *Sam Peckinpah*. Sp: Harry Julian Fink, Oscar Saul, and Peckinpah. Cast: Richard Harris, Jim Hutton, James Coburn, Michael Anderson Jr., Senta Berger, Mario Adorf, Brock Peters, Warren Oates, Ben Johnson, R.G. Armstrong, L.Q. Jones, Slim Pickens, Dub Taylor, Michael Pate, and John Davis Chandler.

29. THE AGONY AND THE ECSTASY. 20th Century-Fox, 1965 (c). *Carol Reed*. Sp: Philip Dunne, b/o novel by Irving Stone. Cast: Rex Harrison, Diane Cilento, Harry Andrews, Albert Lupo, Adolfo Celi, Venantino Venantini, John Stacy, Fausto Tozzi, and Tomas Milian.

30. THE WAR LORD. Universal, 1965 (c). *Franklin Schaffner*. Sp: John Collier and Millard Kaufman, b/o play by Leslie Stevens. Cast: Richard Boone, Rosemary Forsyth, Maurice Evans, Guy Stockwell, Niall MacGinnis, Henry Wilcoxon, James Farentino, and Michael Conrad.

31. KHARTOUM. United Artists, 1966 (c). *Basil Dearden*. Sp: Robert Ardrey. Cast: Laurence Olivier, Richard Johnson, Ralph Richardson, Alexander Knox, Johnny Sekka, Michael Hordern, Nigel Green, Hugh Williams, and Peter Arne.

32. COUNTERPOINT. Universal, 1967 (c). *Ralph Nelson*. Sp: James Lee and Joel Oliansky, b/o novel by Alan Sillitoe. Cast: Maximilian Schell, Kathryn Hays, Leslie Nielsen, Anton Diffring, Linden Chiles, Pete Masterson, Curt Lowens, Neva Patterson, Cyril Delevanti, and Parley Baer.

33. PLANET OF THE APES. 20th Century-Fox, 1968 (c). *Franklin J. Schaffner*. Sp: Michael Wilson and Rod Serling, b/o novel by Pierre Boulle. Cast: Roddy McDowall, Kim Hunter, Maurice Evans, James Whitmore, James Daly, Linda Harrison, Robert Gunner, Lou Wagner, Woodrow Parfrey, and Jeff Burton.

34. WILL PENNY. Paramount, 1968 (c). *Tom Gries*. Sp: Gries. Cast: Joan Hackett, Donald Pleasence, Lee Majors, Bruce Dern, Ben Johnson, Slim Pickens, Clifton James, Anthony Zerbe, Jon Francis, Roy Jenson, G.D. Spraldin, Quentin Dean, William Schallert, and Lydia Clarke.

35. NUMBER ONE. United Artists, 1969 (c). *Tom Gries*. Sp: David Moessinger. Cast: Jessica Walter, Bruce Dern, John Randolph, Diana Muldaur, G.D. Spradlin, Richard Elkins, Mike Henry, Steve Franken, Al Hirt, and the New Orleans Saints.

36. BENEATH THE PLANET OF THE APES. 20th Century-Fox, 1970 (c). *Ted Post*. Sp: Paul Dehn, b/o story by Dehn and Mort Abrahams, from characters created by Pierre Boulle. Cast: James Franciscus, Kim Hunter, Maurice Evans, Linda Harrison, Paul Richards, Victor Buono, James Gregory, Jeff Corey, Natalie Trundy, Thomas Gomez, David Watson, and Gregory Sierra.

37.   THE HAWAIIANS. United Artists, 1970 (c). *Tom Gries.* Sp: James R. Webb, b/o novel by James A. Michener. Cast: Geraldine Chaplin, John Philip Law, Tina Chen, Alec McCowen, Mako, Don Knight, Miko Mayama, Virginia Ann Lee, Naomi Stevens, and Harry Townes.

38.   JULIUS CAESAR. American International, 1970 (c). *Stuart Burge.* Sp: Robert Furnival, b/o play by William Shakespeare. Cast: Jason Robards, John Gielgud, Richard Johnson, Robert Vaughn, Richard Chamberlain, Diana Rigg, Jill Bennett, Christopher Lee, and Alan Browning.

39.   THE OMEGA MAN. Warner Brothers, 1971 (c). *Boris Sagal.* Sp: John William and Joyce H. Corrington, b/o novel by Richard Matheson. Cast: Anthony Zerbe, Rosalind Cash, Paul Koslo, Lincoln Kilpatrick, and Eric Laneuville. Previously filmed as *The Last Man on Earth* (1964).

40.   ANTONY AND CLEOPATRA. Rank, 1972 (c). *Charleton Heston.* Sp: Heston, b/o play by William Shakespeare. Cast: Hildegarde Neil, Eric Porter, John Castle, Fernando Rey, Freddie Jones, and Roger Delgardo.

41.   SKYJACKED. MGM, 1972 (c). *John Guillermin.* Sp: Stanley R. Greenberg, b/o novel by David Harper. Cast: Yvette Mimieux, James Brolin, Claude Akins, Jeanne Crain, Susan Dey, Roosevelt Grier, Mariette Hartley, Walter Pidgeon, Mike Henry, Ken Swofford, Nicholas Hammond, and Leslie Uggams.

42.   CALL OF THE WILD. Intercontinental Releasing Corp., 1973 (c). *Ken Annakin.* Sp: Hubert Frank and Tibor Reves, b/o novel by Jack London. Cast: Raimund Harmsdorf, Michele Mercier, George Eastman, and Sancho Garcia. Previously filmed in 1923 and 1935.

43.   SOYLENT GREEN. MGM, 1973 (c). *Richard Fleischer.* Sp: Stanley R. Greenberg, b/o novel by Harry Harrison. Cast: Leigh Taylor-Young, Chuck Connors, Joseph Cotten, Brock Peters, Paula Kelly, Edward G. Robinson, Mike Henry, Whit Bissell, and Celia Lovsky.

44.   THE THREE MUSKETEERS. 20th Century-Fox, 1974 (c). *Richard Lester.* Sp: George MacDonald Fraser, b/o book by Alexandre Dumas. Cast: Oliver Reed, Raquel Welch, Faye Dunaway, Richard Chamberlain, Michael York, Frank Finlay, Geraldine Chaplin, Christopher Lee, Simon Ward, Jean-Pierre Cassell, Roy Kinnear, and Spike Milligan. Other versions filmed in 1914, 1921, 1935, 1939 and 1948.

45. AIRPORT 1975. Universal, 1974 (c). *Jack Smight*. Sp: Don Ingalls, suggested by novel by Arthur Hailey. Cast: Karen Black, Gloria Swanson, George Kennedy, Susan Clark, Myrna Loy, Efrem Zimbalist Jr., Dana Andrews, Helen Reddy, Linda Blair, Roy Thinnes, Sid Caesar, Ed Nelson, Nancy Olson, and Martha Scott.

46. EARTHQUAKE. Universal, 1974 (c). *Mark Robson*. Sp: George Fox and Mario Puzo. Cast: Ava Gardner, George Kennedy, Lorne Greene, Genevieve Bujold, Richard Roundtree, Marjoe Gortner, Barry Sullivan, Lloyd Nolan, Victoria Principal, Walter Matuschanskayasky (Matthau), Monica Lewis, Gabriel Dell, and John Randolph.

47. THE FOUR MUSKETEERS. 20th Century-Fox, 1975 (c). *Richard Lester*. Sp: George MacDonald Fraser, b/o book by Alexandre Dumas. Cast: Oliver Reed, Raquel Welch, Faye Dunaway, Richard Chamberlain, Michael York, Frank Finlay, Geraldine Chaplin, Christopher Lee, Simon Ward, Jean-Pierre Cassell, and Roy Kinnear.

48. MIDWAY. Universal, 1976 (c). *Jack Smight*. Sp: Donald S. Sanford. Cast: Henry Fonda, James Coburn, Glenn Ford, Hal Holbrook, Toshiro Mifune, Robert Mitchum, Cliff Robertson, and Robert Wagner.

49. THE LAST HARD MEN. 20th Century-Fox, 1976 (c). *Andrew V. McLaglen*. Sp: Guerdon Trueblood, b/o novel by Brian Garfield. Cast: James Coburn, Barbara Hershey, Christopher Mitchum, Jorge Rivero, Michael Parks, Larry Wilcox, Morgan Paull, and Thalmus Rasulala.

50. TWO-MINUTE WARNING. Universal, 1976 (c). *Larry Peerce*. Sp: Edward Hume, b/o novel by George LaFountaine. Cast: John Cassavetes, Martin Balsam, Beau Bridges, Marilyn Hassett, David Janssen, Jack Klugman, Gena Rowlands, and Joe Kapp.

51. THE PRINCE AND THE PAUPER. An Alexander Salkind Production, 1977 (c). *Richard Fleischer*. Sp: George MacDonald Fraser, b/o script by Berta Dominguez and Pierre Spengler. Cast: George C. Scott, Raquel Welch, Rex Harrison, Ernest Borgnine, Mark Lester, and Oliver Reed. Previously filmed in 1909, 1915, 1923, 1937, 1962.

52. GRAY LADY DOWN. Universal, 1977 (c). *David Greene*. Sp: James Whittaker.

INDEX

Adams, Julie, 53
Agony and the Ecstasy, The, 95-96, 98
Airport, 134
Airport 1975, 12, 134-135, 136
Along Came Jones (TV), 54
Ambler, Eric, 76
Anatomy of a Murder, 80
Anderson, James, 41
Anderson, Judith, 61, 102
Anderson, Michael, 76
Andrews, Dana, 134, 135
Angel Street (stage), 24
Annakin, Ken, 123
Ansara, Michael, 90
Antony and Cleopatra (film), 112, 120, 123
Antony and Cleopatra (stage), 24
Archerd, Army, 104
Ardrey, Robert, 101
Arliss, George, 12
Arrowhead, 45

Bad For Each Other, 47
Badge of Evil (Masterson), 65
Bailout at 43,000 (TV), 54
Baker, Carroll, 69, 70, 92
Balsam, Martin, 140
Bancroft, Anne, 120
Baxter, Anne, 61, 62
Bayer, William, 69
Begley, Ed, 28
Beneath the Planet of the Apes, 112
Ben-Hur, 11, 72, 74, 76, 78, 80, 81, 103, 130
Bennett, Jill, 115
Berney, William, 27
Bettger, Lyle, 36
Bickford, Charles, 69, 70
Big Country, The, 69-71, 74
Black, Karen, 134
Bloom, Claire, 72
Boehm, Sydney, 36, 49
Bolt, Robert, 98
Borgnine, Ernest, 140
Boulle, Pierre, 103
Boyd, Stephen, 76
Boyer, Charles, 72
Bradley, David, 17, 19, 24, 26, 115
Brandon, Henry, 43
Bridges, Beau, 140
Brolin, James, 123

Bronston, Samuel, 81, 84, 87, 90
Brynner, Yul, 61, 71
Buccaneer, The, 44, 71-72, 74
Bujold, Genevieve, 130, 131
Burge, Stuart, 115

Caesar, Sid, 134
Call of the Wild, 123
Canutt, Yakima, 74, 81
Carter, Alan (brother), 15
Carter, Lilla (sister), 15
Carter, Russell (father), 15
Cassavetes, John, 140
Cassell, Jean-Pierre, 129
Cassidy, Hopalong, 111
Castle, John, 120
Chamberlain, Richard, 127
Chambers, John, 103
Chaplin, Geraldine, 127
Chapman, John, 26
Charlton, Lilla (mother), 15
Charlton, Percy (great uncle), 15
Chen, Tina, 112
Christie, Julie, 98
Christmas Carol, A, 17
Citizen Kane, 62
Clark, Susan, 134
Clarke, Lydia. *See* Heston, Lydia Clarke
"Climax" (TV), 54
Coburn, James, 95, 139
Cock-a-Doodle-Doo (stage), 26
Collier, John, 98
Connors, Chuck, 69, 126
Cooper, Gary, 51, 54, 76
Cordell, Frank, 101
Cornell, Katharine, 24
Cosby, Bill, 111
Cotten, Joseph, 126
Counterpoint, 102
Cousins, Margaret, 54
Crowded Sky, The, 135
Crowther, Bosley, 28
Crucible, The, (stage), 125

Daly, James, 107
Danova, Cesare, 74
Darby's Rangers, 62
Dark City, 28, 30
Day in Town, A, (TV), 54

Dearden, Basil, 101
DeCarlo, Yvonne, 61
DeFore, Don, 28
Dehn, Paul, 112
Demarest, William, 54
DeMille, Cecil B., 30, 32, 34, 36, 44, 47, 56, 57, 59, 61, 62, 71, 72
Derek, John, 61
Design for a Stained Glass Window (stage), 27
Detective Story (stage), 27
Diamond Head, 84, 87
Dieterle, William, 28
Disney, Walt, 103
Donlevy, Brian, 84
Downs, Donald, 84
Dumas, Alexander, 127, 129
Dunaway, Faye, 127
Dunne, Philip, 95, 96

Earthquake, 11, 130-131, 134, 136
Easter Dinner, The (Downes), 84
Eastman, George, 123
El Cid, 12, 81-82
Elizabeth the Queen (TV), 102
Emmons, Della Gould, 52
Enemy of the People, An, 135
Evans, Maurice, 107, 112
Evelyn, Judith, 29

Far Horizons, The, 52
Ferrer, José, 92
Fiedler, John, 26
55 Days at Peking, 12, 87, 90
Fink, Harry Julian, 92
Finlay, Frank, 127
Fitz-Richard, Arthur, 38
Fleischer, Richard, 126
Fleming, Rhonda, 43
Foch, Nina, 61
Fonda, Henry, 62, 139
Ford, Glenn, 139
Ford, Wallace, 54
Foreman, L. L., 36
Forsyth, Rosemary, 98
Foster, Dianne, 47
Four Musketeers, The, 129, 136
Fox, George, 131
Franciscus, James, 112

Frank, Fredric M., 34, 81
Frank, Hubert, 123
Fraser, George MacDonald, 127
Fraser, John, 82
Frings, Ketti, 28
From Here to Eternity, 47
Fry, Christopher, 74, 80

Gable, Clark, 71
Gardner, Ava, 87, 130, 131
Garfield, Brian, 139
Garland, Robert, 27
Garner, James, 62
General, The (Sillitoe), 102
Gerber, Ella, 27
Gielgud, John, 115
Gilman, Peter, 87
Glass Menagerie, The (play), 24
Gone With the Wind, 38
Gordon, Bernard, 87
Gordon, Bruce, 24
Gortner, Marjoe, 130
Grahame, Gloria, 36
Grainer, Ron, 118
Grant, Cary, 51, 52, 81, 82
Grant, James Edward, 62
Gray, Coleen, 26
Gray Lady Down, 140
Greatest Show on Earth, The, 12, 32, 34, 36, 49, 54, 57, 72
Greatest Story Ever Told, The, 90, 92
Great Movies, The (Bayer), 69
Greenberg, Stanley R., 123, 126
Greene, Lorne, 130
Green, Guy, 87
Gries, Tom, 107, 109, 111, 112
Griffith, Hugh, 76, 80
Gruber, Frank, 43
Guardino, Harry, 84
Guillermin, John, 123
Guinness, Alec, 127
Gulliver's Travels, 104

Hackett, Joan, 107
Hailey, Arthur, 134
"Hallmark Hall of Fame" (TV), 90, 102
Hamilton, Donald, 70
Harareet, Haya, 76
Hardy, Joseph, 125

Harper, David, 123
Harris, Richard, 95, 112, 115
Harris, Rosemary, 78
Harrison, Harry, 126
Harrison, Linda, 112
Harrison, Rex, 95, 140
Hart, Richard, 26
Haskin, Byron, 47
Hassett, Marilyn, 140
Hawaii, 112
Hawaiians, The, 112, 115
Hawkins, Jack, 76
Hayes, Joseph, 26
Hayward, Susan, 44, 45, 49, 80
Head, Edith, 54
Heggen, Thomas, 62
Hershey, Barbara, 139
Heston, Chester (stepfather), 15
Heston, Fraser (son), 61
Heston, Holly Ann (daughter), 84
Heston, Lydia Clarke (wife), 19, 22, 24, 27,
    41, 47, 57, 78, 84, 98
Holbrook, Hal, 139
Holden, William, 28
Hopper, Jerry, 43, 51, 52
Hovey, Tim, 53
Hume, Edward, 140
Hunter, Jeffrey, 26
Hunter, Kim, 107, 112
Hutton, Betty, 34

I Am Legend (Matheson), 115
Ibsen, Henrik, 135
Ingalls, Don, 134
Innes, Hammond, 76
Ireland, John, 87, 90, 136
Ivanhoe, 81
Ives, Burl, 69, 70

Jacobs, Arthur P., 103, 112
Jane Eyre (TV), 27
Janssen, David, 140
Jaws, 135
John Loves Mary (stage), 24
Johnson, Richard, 115
Jones, Jennifer, 38, 41, 54
Jordon, Richard, 136
Julius Caesar, 26, 27, 115

Klugman, Jack, 140
Kaufman, Millard, 98
Keller, Harry, 65
Kennedy, George, 130, 134
Khartoum, 101
Kirk, Lisa, 29
Kiss and Tell (stage), 24

La Fountaine, George, 139
Lancaster, Burt, 45, 47
Landau, Ely, 135
Lange, Hope, 62
Last Angry Man, The, 80
Last Hard Men, The, 139
Last Man on Earth, The, 115
Leaf and Bough (stage), 26
Leavitt, Sam, 87
Lee, James, 102
Leigh, Janet, 65
"Leiningen Versus the Ants" (short story),
    47
Lester, Mark, 140
Lester, Richard, 127, 129
Let's Make Love, 78
Levin, Henry, 45
Levy, Benn W., 78
Lindfors, Viveca, 28
Liss, Joseph, 29
Lives of the Hunted (Seton), 19
Logan, Joshua, 62
London, Jack, 123
Longest Day, The, 139
Loren, Sophia, 81, 82, 84
Lovers, The (stage), 98
Loy, Myrna, 134
Lucas, John Meredyth, 28
Lucy Gallant, 54
Lukas, Paul, 87
Lyndon, Barre, 34

Macbeth (film), 24
Macbeth (stage), 78, 136
Macbeth (TV), 29
McClintic, Guthrie, 24
McCoy, Horace, 45, 47
MacDougall, Ranald, 47, 49
McDowall, Roddy, 107
McGavin, Darren, 26

McLaglen, Andrew V., 139
MacMurray, Fred, 52
Mahin, John Lee, 54
Major Dundee, 92, 94-95
Malden, Karl, 38
Mamoulian, Rouben, 26
Man For All Seasons, A (stage), 98, 101
Mann, Anthony, 81
Man in the Shadow, 62
March, Fredric, 71
Marcus, Larry, 28
Marquand, John P., 62
Marshall, George, 11, 36
Martinelli, Elsa, 84
Martin, Pete, 29, 74
Marton, Andrew, 74
Masterson, Whit, 65
Maté, Rudolph, 52, 62
Matheson, Richard, 115
Matthau, Walter, 130
Maurey, Nicole, 51
Mazurki, Mike, 28
"Medallion Theatre" (TV), 54
Meeker, Ralph, 17
Michener, James, 112, 115
Midway, 136, 139
Mifune, Toshiro, 139
Miller, Arthur, 125
Miller, Winston, 52, 54
Mimieux, Yvette, 87
Mineo, Sal, 53, 92
Mister Roberts (stage), 62
Mitchell, Thomas, 51
Mitchum, Christopher, 139
Mitchum, Robert, 139
Moessinger, David, 111
Moffat, Donald, 78
Moffitt, Jack, 51
Monroe, Marilyn, 78
Montand, Yves, 78
Moon, Lynne Sue, 90
Moross, Jerome, 71
Morrow, Susan, 38
Muldaur, Diana, 111
Muni, Paul, 12, 80
Murphy, George, 102

Naked Jungle, The, 12, 47, 49, 62
Neal, Patricia, 17

Neil, Hildegarde, 120
Nelson, Ralph, 102
Niven, David, 87
North, Alex, 96
North, Edmund H., 52
Number One, 111, 123

Of Human Bondage (TV), 27
Oliansky, Joel, 102
Oliver Twist, 17
Olivier, Laurence, 41, 78, 101, 120
Olson, James, 125
Omega Man, The, 118, 120, 123, 126
Oursler, Fulton, 90

Page, Genevieve, 81
Pal, George, 47, 49
Palance, Jack, 45
Papas, Irene, 120
Parker, Eleanor, 47, 49
Parks, Michael, 139
Parrish, Robert, 54
Patrick, John, 44
Patriots, The (TV), 90
Payne, John, 54
Peck, Gregory, 69, 70
Peckinpah, Sam, 92, 94, 95
Peer Gynt, 17, 19
Peerce, Larry, 140
Peters, Brock, 95
"Philco Playhouse" (TV), 29
Pigeon That Took Rome, The, 84
Planet of the Apes, 12, 103-4, 107
"Playhouse 90" (TV), 62
Pleasence, Donald, 107
Point of No Return (TV), 62
Poitier, Sidney, 92
Pony Express, 43, 44
Porter, Eric, 120
Post, Ted, 112
President's Lady, The, 43-45, 49, 71
Presley, Elvis, 82
Price, Vincent, 61, 115
Prince and the Pauper, The, 140
Private War of Major Benson, The, 52, 57, 87
Puzo, Mario, 131

Quinn, Anthony, 72

s, Claude, 92
ndall, Stuart, 43
Rapper, Irving, 47
Ray, Nicholas, 87
Reagan, Ronald, 102
Reddy, Helen, 134
Redgrave, Vanessa, 135-36

Reed, Carol, 95
Reed, Donna, 52
Reed, Oliver, 127, 140
Reves, Tibor, 123
Reed, Oliver, 127, 140
Reves, Tibor, 123
Rey, Fernando, 120
Richards, Beah, 125
Richards, Sylvia, 38
Richardson, Howard, 27
Richardson, Ralph, 101
Rigg, Diana, 115
Ritter, Thelma, 54
Rivero, Jorge, 139
Robards, Jason, 115
Robe, The, 45
"Robert Montgomery Presents" (TV), 54
Roberts, Marguerite, 87
Roberts, William, 52
Robertson, Cliff, 139
Robinson, Edward G., 61, 104, 107, 126
Robson, Flora, 87
Robson, Mark, 130, 131
Rogers, Roy, 111
Roland, Gilbert, 62
Roundtree, Richard, 130
Rowlands, Gena, 140
Rozsa, Miklos, 80, 81
Ruby Gentry, 38, 41, 54

Sagal, Boris, 118
St. John, Theodore, 34
Salkind, Ilya, 127, 129, 130
Samson and Delilah, 57
Sanford, Donald S., 139
Saul, Oscar, 92
Savage, The, 11, 36, 38, 41
Savalas, Terry, 92
Scalpel (McCoy), 45
Schaefer, George, 90
Schaffner, Franklin J., 98, 104

Schell, Maximilian, 102
Scott, George C., 140
Scott, Lizabeth, 28, 47
Scott, Martha, 27, 78
Secret of the Incas, 49, 52
Seltzer, Walter, 123
Selznick, David, 38
Serling, Rod, 104
Seton, Ernest Thompson, 19
Seven Year Itch, The (stage), 57
Shamroy, Leon, 98
Shavelson, Melville, 84
Sillitoe, Alan, 102
Simmons, Jean, 69, 70
Simmons, Richard Alan, 53
Sinclair, Mary, 27
Skolsky, Sidney, 19
Skyjacked, 123
Smight, Jack, 134, 139
Smith, Cecil, 101
Snell, Peter, 120
Sondergaard, Gale, 125
Sothern, Hugh, 44
Soylent Green, 14, 125-126
Squire, Katherine, 26
Stapleton, Maureen, 24
State of the Union (stage), 24, 78
Stephenson, Carl, 47
Sterling, Jan, 43
Stevens, George, 90, 92
Stevens, Inger, 72
Stevens, Leslie, 98
Stewart, James, 36, 80
Stone, Irving, 44, 95
Stone, Milburn, 38, 59
"Studio One" (TV), 27, 29
Sullivan, Dan, 125, 136
"Suspense" (TV), 29
Swanson, Gloria, 134
Swenson, Inga, 125
Sydow, Max von, 92

Taming of the Shrew, The (TV), 29
Tamiroff, Akim, 65
Taylor-Young, Leigh, 126
Ten Commandments, The, 11, 57, 61, 62, 72, 92, 130
"Terry and the Pirates" (radio), 17
Thomas, Bob, 115

Thor, Jerome, 90
Three Friends, The, 17
Three Musketeers, The, 12, 127, 129, 136
Three Violent People, 62
Tiomkin, Dimitri, 90
Tora! Tora! Tora!, 139
Touch of Evil, 11, 65, 69
Treasure Island, 17
Tree, Iris, 26
Trevor, Claire, 54
Trueblood, Guerdon, 139
Tryon, Tom, 62
Tucker, Forrest, 43, 62
Tumbler, The (stage), 78
Tunberg, Karl, 74, 80
Twain, Mark, 140
Two-Minute Warning, 139-40

Vidor, King, 38, 41

Wagner, Robert, 139
Wallace, Irving, 47
Wallace, Lew, 74
Wallach, Eli, 24
Wallis, Hal, 27, 28, 30, 45
Walter, Jessica, 111
War Lord, The, 14, 98, 111
Warren, Charles Marquis, 43, 45
Watts, Richard, Jr., 78

Wayne, John, 51, 81, 92, 111
Webb, Jack, 28
Webb, James R., 112
Welch, Raquel, 127, 140
Welles, Orson, 11, 17, 62, 65, 69, 120
White, David, 26
Whitmore, James, 107
Whittaker, James, 140
Wilcoxon, Henry, 72
Wilde, Cornel, 34
Will Penny, 12, 107, 109, 111, 123
Wilson, Michael, 104
Wood, Peter, 136
Wreck of the Mary Deare, The, 76, 78
Wuthering Heights (TV), 27
Wyler, William, 14, 69, 71, 74, 76
Wyman, Jane, 54
Wynn, Ed, 92

Yordan, Philip, 47, 81, 87
York, Michael, 127
You Can't Take It With You (stage), 24
Young, Robert, 51

Zanuck, Darryl, 45
Zanuck, Richard, 103
Zerbe, Anthony, 118
Zimbalist, Efrem Jr., 134, 135
Zugsmith, Albert, 11, 62, 65

ABOUT THE AUTHOR

Michael B. Druxman, a Hollywood publicist, is the author of biographies on Paul Muni, Basil Rathbone, and Merv Griffin, as well as *Make It Again, Sam: A Survey of Movie Remakes*. He resides in Agoura, California.

ABOUT THE EDITOR

Ted Sennett is the author of *Warner Brothers Presents,* a tribute to the great Warners films of the thirties and forties, and of *Lunatics and Lovers,* on the long-vanished but well-remembered "screwball" movie comedies of the past. He is also the editor of *The Movie Buff's Book* and has written about films for magazines and newspapers. He lives in New Jersey with his wife and three children.